21
世纪经济管理类精品教材

外贸英语函电

（第4版）

王 虹 耿 伟◎主 编

English for International
Trade Communication

清华大学出版社
北 京

内 容 简 介

"外贸英语函电"是一门以对外经贸商务活动的成交过程为主线,将英语与国际贸易业务环节相结合的课程。作为该课程的配套教材,本书介绍了国际贸易实务中各种英文业务函件及电子邮件的写作格式和表达方法,以及对外贸易各环节的具体做法,还介绍了跨境电子商务的相关知识,旨在提高学生英语水平的同时,使其熟练掌握国际贸易实务中常用的基本术语及表达技巧。本书共有 18 个单元,系统介绍了英文商务信函写作的基本知识,以及相关的业务关系建立、询盘和发盘、订单及其履行、支付、包装、装运、保险、争议和索赔、跨境电子商务等内容。

本书既适合国际经济与贸易专业的学生学习使用,也可作为国际贸易从业人员的参考用书。

图书在版编目(CIP)数据

外贸英语函电 / 王虹,耿伟主编. —4 版. —北京:清华大学出版社,2021.5(2024.8重印)

21 世纪经济管理类精品教材

ISBN 978-7-302-58166-6

I. ①外… II. ①王… ②耿… III. ①对外贸易-英语-电报信函-写作-高等学校-教材 IV. ①F75

中国版本图书馆 CIP 数据核字(2021)第 088817 号

责任编辑:邓 婷
封面设计:刘 超
版式设计:文森时代
责任校对:马军令
责任印制:丛怀宇

出版发行:清华大学出版社
　　　　网　　址:https://www.tup.com.cn, https://www.wqxuetang.com
　　　　地　　址:北京清华大学学研大厦 A 座　　　　　　邮　　编:100084
　　　　社 总 机:010-83470000　　　　　　　　　　　　邮　　购:010-62786544
　　　　投稿与读者服务:010-62776969, c-service@tup.tsinghua.edu.cn
　　　　质量反馈:010-62772015, zhiliang@tup.tsinghua.edu.cn
印 装 者:三河市少明印务有限公司
经　　销:全国新华书店
开　　本:185mm×260mm　　　印　　张:15　　　字　　数:486 千字
版　　次:2009 年 8 月第 1 版　　2021 年 5 月第 4 版　　印　　次:2024 年 8 月第 6 次印刷
定　　价:49.80 元

产品编号:089006-01

再版前言

"外贸英语函电"是国际经济与贸易专业及商务英语专业的核心专业课程之一，是一门将英语与国际贸易业务环节相结合的课程。本书介绍了国际贸易实务中各种英文业务函件及电子邮件的写作格式和表达方法，以及对外贸易各环节的具体做法，旨在提高学生英语水平的同时，使其熟练掌握国际贸易实务中常用的基本术语及表达技巧，培养和强化其外贸业务工作能力，为国家培养从事国际贸易工作的高水平"应用型"人才。

本书主要特点是：①以对外经贸商务活动的成交过程为主线；②信函范例精选国际贸易活动的最新材料和实例；③突出基本词汇、句型和格式，有助于读者撰写规范的国际贸易函电；④练习形式多样，针对性强，培养学生学以致用的能力；⑤每章设置有背景介绍、写作模块等内容，体现了对外贸易发展的实际情况，便于课堂教学和自学。

本书于 2009 年出版第 1 版，2013 年出版第 2 版，2017 年出版第 3 版，本次所出版为第 4 版。为了满足我国对外经济贸易不断发展的需要，特别是在经济全球化背景下对外经济贸易面临的新形势，笔者对各单元内容做了相应的增减和更替，但各部分的宗旨和侧重点未做更改，笔者对贸易业务磋商过程中各个环节的函电例文进行了必要的增删和系统的修改，删去了前几版中一些过时的表达和书写格式；对每一单元后的常用例句也做了修改，删掉了过时的例句，增加了新颖实用的例句。第 4 版在原有跨境电子商务相关信函的基础上，增加了跨境电子商务物流仓储的相关信函，以跟上时代发展的步伐，与时俱进。

本书共有 18 个单元。第 1 单元系统介绍了英文商务信函写作的基本知识，第 2 至第 17 单元遵循对外贸易常规流程，依次介绍建立业务关系、询盘、发盘、还盘、达成业务关系、支付条款、信用证的开立与修改、包装与唛头、装运、保险、代理、抗议与索赔、促销、跨境电子商务、国际贸易合同的写作、合同与协议等内容，第 18 章简要介绍了其他常用商务信函的写作技巧。此外，各单元练习题的参考答案可通过扫描相应的二维码来获取。同时，我们会为选择本书作教材的教师提供电子课件。

本书由王虹和耿伟担任主编并负责全书的统稿工作，具体编写分工为：第 1 单元由耿伟、李伟编写；第 2、3、4 单元由李伟、刘晓茜编写；第 5、6 单元由冯雅荻编写；第 7、8 单元由贾兴兴编写；第 9 单元由王虹、崔美英编写；第 10、11 单元由马林林编写；第 12、13、14 单元由李康宁、袁堃编写；第 15 单元由崔美英编写；第 16、17、18 单元由王曼、袁堃编写。

受编写时间和作者水平所限，书中难免存在不妥之处，敬请同人和广大读者不吝赐教。

编　者
2021 年 3 月

目　录

CONTENTS

Chapter 1   Business Letters

1.1   Introduction

Business letter is the most frequently used form of communication. It is very important in the business world. Business executives are supposed to write good business letters as to carry out business routine efficiently. If a businessman is unable to write an effective business letter, it is very difficult to represent himself positively, which may cause some problems in doing business.

All business letters have two main functions. One is to ask for and give a reply to an inquiry, offer, order or complaint. The other one is to keep a record of all the important facts for ready reference. An effective business letter will say what the writer wants it to say clearly and simply. It should be precise, straightforward, relevant and action-centered. It should also be written in a friendly and formal style using plain language. Thus, in order to communicate effectively, you should ensure that the letters portray you as approachable, caring, effective and professional. In addition, you should be very familiar with the established layout and practice of business letters. There are three styles of business communication: the blocked style, the indented style and the semi-blocked style. The blocked style with open punctuation is the most popular method of display for business letters, because it is considered to be businesslike, simple and professional.

The business letter can tell readers a lot about the writer and the writer's company. A business letter that is neat, easy to read, and presents a professional image will leave a good impression on the reader. Such a letter helps the writer as much as the reader, and will probably mean an earlier reply. In today's global market place, the reader's first impression often comes from the appearance of the documents and the quality of the paper. So you should pay some attention to the paper quality, the paper color, the paper size and margins. Firstly, never use paper that is too flimsy. Secondly, white is the standard color for business purposes, although light colors such as gray and ivory are sometimes used. Thirdly, the size of papers varies slightly from country to country. In the United States, the standard paper size for business documents is 8.5 by 11 inches. Last but not least, the document is to be centered in the page, leaving at least one-inch margins all around. We can use word-processing software to achieve the balance by defining the format.

This chapter is intended to develop skills in writing good business letters. It contains guidelines on developing personal writing style, using appropriate tone and composing effective communications in modern business language.

1.2   Writing Guide

1.2.1   The Essentials of Business Letter Writing

Since the main purpose of business correspondence is to convey a message, the letter should be written in language that is easily understood. The writer must make sure that it should be free from grammatical blemishes, and also free from the slightest possibility of being misunderstood. There are certain essential qualities of business letters, which can be summed up in the following 7 "Cs" principles.

1. Clarity

You must try to express yourself clearly, so that the reader can understand. To achieve this, you should keep in mind the purpose of the letter and use appropriate words in correct sentence structures to convey your meanings. We should also avoid ambiguous sentences. Otherwise, the business letter will cause trouble to both sides. All in all, good, straightforward and simple language are needed for business letters.

2. Conciseness

Conciseness means saying things in the fewest possible words. The elimination of wordy business jargon can help to make a letter clearer and at the same time more concise. If conciseness conflicts with courtesy, then make a little sacrifice of conciseness. Generally speaking, to achieve conciseness, one should try to avoid wordiness or redundancy.

3. Courtesy

Courtesy is not mere politeness. It should hardly be necessary to stress the importance of courtesy in your letters. One of the most important things is promptness. Punctuality will please your customer who dislikes waiting for days before he gets a reply to his letter. Differences are bound to occur in business, but with diplomacy and tact they can be overcome and settled without offence on either side. Remember that it's nearly always wrong to doubt a statement made in good faith by the other side and even worse to contradict it. In letters we should always keep in mind the person we are writing to, see things from his point of view, visualize him in his surroundings, see his problems and difficulties and express our ideas in terms of his experience.

4. Consideration

Consideration emphasizes You-attitude rather than We-attitude. When writing a letter, keep the reader's requests, needs, desires, as well as his feelings in mind. Plan the best way to present the message for the reader to receive.

5. Correctness

Correctness here refers to appropriate and grammatically correct language, factual information and accurate reliable figures, as well as the right forms and conventions. All facts should be checked and double checked. Special attention should also be paid to name of goods, specification, quantity, figure, unit, etc.

6. Concreteness

To make the message specific, definite and vivid is the key point of concreteness. The writer must ensure that the letter contains all the information the recipient needs to act upon. Put yourself in reader's place. It is necessary to check the message carefully before it is sent out.

7. Completeness

Like any other letter, a good business letter should be complete, providing all the information and data necessary for a specific issue. If any necessary piece of information is lacking, the reader will have to ask for clarification, which means that you will have to write another letter. It will not only waste time, energy and money, but also damage the image of your company.

1.2.2　The Structure of Business Letters

Business letter has its special formats. In the formal business letters, we usually use 12 factors. They are letterhead, reference number, date, inside address, attention line, salutation, subject line, body, complimentary close, signature, IEC block, postscript. Among them, letterhead, date, inside address, salutation, body, complimentary close and signature belong to the standard factors and must be contained in the formal business letters. Whether to use other factors depends on the specific situation. The approximate locations of these factors in a business letter are as follows:

Letterhead

Reference number

Date

Inside address

_____
_____

　　　　Attention line

Salutation

Subject line

Body

_____

_____

_____

_____

_____

_____

_____

Complimentary close

Signature

IEC block

Postscript

While the horizontal placement of letter parts may vary, the vertical order of these parts is standard. The followings are the most common components and formats.

1. The Basic Components of Business Letters

1) Letterhead

For letters to outsiders, many companies use letterhead stationery which is professionally printed at the top of the page, though some are printed at the bottom or even at the upper-left corner of the page. The letterhead indicates the name, address, telephone, fax number and E-mail address of the company sending the letter. It helps the recipient to identify the company from which the sender comes just at a glance. If letterhead stationery is not available, you can type the heading, which includes a return address, and leaves about a two-inch top margin.

2) Date

Writing date in English goes in two styles: one is American style, and the other is British style. The standard order of typing the date in the U.S. is month, day, year. For example: September 12, 2018. While in Britain, the standard order is day, month, year. For example: 12 September, 2018. The day can be written or typed in either cardinal numbers (1, 2, 3, 4, etc.) or in ordinal numbers (1st, 2nd, 3rd, 4th, etc.). The month and the year had better not be written in their abbreviation forms, otherwise, it may easily cause confusion. For example, 12/09/2018 in the U.S. would mean December 9, 2018, while in Britain it means 12 September, 2018. There is no rule for the date placement. If you use letterhead stationery, place the date one to three blank lines beneath the letterhead. If without letterhead, place the date immediately below the return address.

3) Inside Address

Generally, the inside address should include some or all parts of the following: the name of the recipient, the department name, company name, suite or room number, street address, city, postcode, state/province and country. Of all these parts, postcode is very important, it helps to facilitate mechanical mail-sorting. The inside address appear on the left margin and usually start two to four lines below the date. They appear exactly the same way as on the envelope.

If the receiver of the letter is in the U.S., the address also includes the name of the state which must be typed in capitalized two letter abbreviation followed by ZIP code. The same way is also used for the provinces and territories in Canadian address.

Precede the addressee's name with a courtesy title (such as Mr., Ms. or Dr.). If you do not know whether the person is a man or a woman, and you have no way to find out, omit the courtesy title and give the full name.

The person's job title can be placed on the same line of the person's name, or on the line below. Try to square the address as much as possible. If the title appears on the same line, place a comma between the name and the title. If it appears on the next line, dispense with the comma. e.g.:

(1) Mr. Dick Eaton, President

(2) Ms. Patricia T. Higgins

   Assistant Vice President

If the name of a specific person is unavailable, you may address the letter to the department, followed by the name of the company. e.g.:

(1) Customer Service Department

   Acme Construction Company

(2) Director of Personnel

   International Trading Co., Ltd.

In order to avoid ambiguity, when you write letters to other countries, always include the name of the country, even if the city mentioned is the country's capital.

The following examples show all the information that may be included in the inside address.

Dr. H. C. Armstrong
Research and Development
Commonwealth Mining Consortium
The Shelton Building, Suite 391
353 Second St. SW
Calgary, AB T2P
Canada

Mr. Thom Collins, President
164 Bay Road
Liquorland
Oklahoma City, OK 73125
U.S.A

4) Salutation

The salutation is the polite greeting with which a letter begins. Place it two lines below the inside address. The salutation should correspond to the first line of the inside address, that is, if the first line of your inside address is a name of a person, the salutation is "Dear + the name". Its form depends upon your relationship with the receiver. The customary formal greeting in a business letter is "Dear Sir" or "Dear Madam" used for addressing one person; and "Dear Sirs", "Dear Mesdames" or "Gentlemen" for addressing two or more people. If the addressee is known to you personally, a warmer greeting such as "Dear Mr. Smith" is preferred. Quite often now companies are owned and/or managed by women, and it is more and more customary to use the greeting: Dear Madam or Sir, if you are not sure whether the letter will be read by a man or a woman. If the addressee is a group, use "Ladies and Gentlemen". Or you may use a polite description, such as "Dear Friends", "Dear SPA supporters". End the salutation with a colon, or a comma.

5) Body

This is the most important part of a letter. It expresses your idea, opinion, purpose and wishes, etc. It usually begins from one or two lines below the salutation. Lines within a paragraph should be single-spaced and double-spaced between paragraphs. There is no strict rule regarding the content of the letter, but it usually includes three parts: the opening paragraph, the middle paragraph and the closing paragraph. The opening paragraph refers to any previous correspondence or introduces the purpose of the letter. The middle paragraph supports the opening and/or provides additional information. The closing paragraph is short and serves as a request, suggestion, or looks to the future. When writing, pay attention to courtesy, clarity, conciseness, consideration, completeness, concreteness and correctness.

6) Complimentary Close

The complimentary close, like the salutation, is purely a matter of custom and a polite way of bringing a letter to a close. It appears one or two lines below the last line of the body. Capitalize the first word and end with a comma. The expression must match the salutation reflecting the relationship between the sender and the receiver of the letter. The main words in complimentary close are as follows: sincerely, faithfully, cordially, respectfully and truly. These words may appear in any of these combinations: Your sincerely, Sincerely yours. The expression used must suit for the occasion.

7) Signature

The writer's signature consists of a handwritten signature and a typewritten signature. Type the name under the complimentary close, leaving enough blank lines (usually leave three blank lines) to sign your name. Never "sign" with a seal or stamp. Then type the signature identification and title. The writer's signature should be placed between the complimentary close and the typed signature.

Sincerely yours,   (signature) Harry Smith

The letterhead indicates that you are representing your company. However, if your letter is on plain paper and you want to emphasize that you are speaking legally for the company, you may type the company's name in capital letters below the complementary close and place the title of the message sender on the same line with or below the typed name.

Very truly yours,   ALVERS, INC (signature) Harry Smith, Project Manager

2. Additional Components of Business Letters

1) Mailing or In-house Notation

Mailing notation shows the specific means of delivery for the convenience of verification. Besides there are two other commonly used forms of mailing notation, e.g. by courier and by EMS. Type them two lines below the date and in all capital letters.

Mailing notations: e.g. "special delivery" "airmail" "registered mail" "certified mail"

In-house notations: e.g. "personal" "confidential".

CONFIDENTIAL

2) Reference

The reference may include a file number, department code or the initials of the signer followed by that of the typist of the letter. Type the reference below the letterhead in short form as "Our ref.:" for the sender's reference, and "Your ref.:" for the recipient's. The purpose of this is to facilitate filing of the letter and link it with previous correspondence.

3) Attention Line

The attention line is used to name the specific individual the letter is addressed to. It is usually placed between the inside address and the salutation or within the inside address and centered over the body of a letter in the indented style. Its abbreviation is Attn. It suggests that the sender hopes the letter receives the immediate attention of a certain person or a specific department.

4) Subject Line/Caption

The subject line is the general idea of a letter. It calls recipients' attention to the topic of the letter. It is often inserted between the salutation and the body of a letter, usually two lines below the salutation. It is also useful as a guide for filing. Some companies omit the word "Subject:", some replace it with "Re:" or "re:" (meaning "regarding"), and some underline the subject line. The following forms are commonly used:

SUBJECT: SALES CONFIRMATION NO. 5678 FOR 300MT OF SOYBEAN OIL

Subject: Sales Confirmation NO. 5678 for 300Metric Tons of Soybean Oil

5) Multiple-page Letter Heading

When typing a multiple-page letter, use letterhead for the first page. The following page or pages should have the same quality, size and color as the first page. The multiple-page heading bears the name of the recipient or his/her organization, the page number, and the date. The following styles are often used for multiple-page letters:

Ms. Katherine Black	Page 2	October 9, 2018

Ms. Katherine Black	-2-	October 9, 2018

Ms. Katherine Black
Page 2
October 6, 2018

6) Reference Initials

Consisting of the signer's initials in capitals followed by a slash or colon followed by the lowercase initials of the person preparing the letter, this item serves as reminder of who prepared the letter. It should be placed at the left margins, two or three lines below the signature. When you type your own letter, don't use initials. When the signature block includes the writer's name, use only the typist's initials. Reference initials are usually given in the form of "author's initials/typist initials", or "author's initials: typist initials".

RS/sm

RS:sm

RS:SM

7) Enclosure Notation

When there is something enclosed with the letter, type the word "Enclosure", or an abbreviation of it(Encl.) in the bottom left-hand, a double spaces under the reference initials, with a figure indicating the number of enclosures, if there are more than one. You can use any of the following styles:

Enclosure

Ence.

Enclosure: 　　1. Purchase Order No. 1234 　　2. Check No. 123

8) Carbon Copy Notation

When you send a copy of the letter to a third person, place a notation directly below the enclosure notation or reference initials. The copy notation is indicated with "CC", or "cc" which is a holdover from the days of carbon copies. Many companies are now using "PC" (for photocopy). e.g.:

　　PC: Margaret Ruth

　　CC: Margaret Ruth

　　cc: Margaret Ruth

9) Postscript/P.S.

If you wish to add something you forget or for emphasis, you may usually add the postscript two lines below the carbon copy notation. Postscript may be preceded by "P. S.", but this is not strictly necessary. In business letters, postscript is not commonly used, while in personal letters, it frequently appears. This item is usually used in the informal styles of letters. The adding of a P.S. should, however, be avoided as far as possible, since it can appear as afterthoughts, indicating a lack of planning. But studies show that postscripts are one of the first things people read and remember, especially when it is handwritten. It sometimes serves the purposes as a message that requires emphasis, or as a personal note. Look at the following example to see where the different parts go in a business letter.

P.S.: You get 5% discount if you book the space by the end of this month.

1.2.3 The Formats of a Business Letter

There are various ways in which the component parts of a business letter can be laid out on the page. Choice of letter format is a matter of individual taste, but it is better to follow established practice, to which the business world has become accustomed. A good plan to make correct practice habit is to adopt one form of letter format and stick to it. The three main formats are as follows.

1. Blocked Format

With this letter style, all letter parts begin at the left margin. Because this style can save the typist's time, so it has come to be much widely used and preferred now. The loss of clarity occasioned by the absence of indentations may be made good by increasing the number of separating line-spacing between paragraphs. The specific layout of letter components in this format are as follows:

LETTERHEAD

Date

Addressee
Inside Address

Salutation:

Re: Blocked Format

This easy-to-type letter is becoming more and more popular and is widely used in many of today's modern offices.

It is a very efficient style because everything begins at the left margins, thereby eliminating the need for tabs.

But critics say it looks somewhat crowded and imbalanced.

Very truly yours,

(Signature)
Typed name

2. Semi-blocked Format

Like blocked format, all letter parts begin at the left margins, except the dateline, complimentary close, company signature and writer's identification, which are set against the right-hand margins. They are placed in this position for filing and reference purposes. It is also named as a modified blocked format. The specific layout of letter components in this style are as follows:

LETTERHEAD

Date

Addressee
Inside Address

Salutation:

Re: Semi-blocked Format

Modified block style has traditionally been the most commonly used of all letter styles.

The most notable difference between this style and the full block is that the date and complimentary close start at the center, or slightly to the right of center.

This letter style is appealing to the eye and is very popular.

Very truly yours

(Signature)
Typed name

3. Indented Format

The indented format may follow the same layout as either the blocked or semi-blocked formats, but will differ in that the paragraphs will each be indented by four or five spaces. It is a traditional format, especially in Britain. The specific layout of letter components in this format are as follows:

LETTERHEAD

Date

Addressee
Inside Address

Salutation:

Re: Indented Format

The distinguishing features of this letter format are that the subject line is indented and all paragraphs are indented too.

It is important to remember that two tabs must be set: one for the date and complimentary close and one for the indentation of the subject line and paragraphs.

This letter style may use more time to type than the previous two.

Very truly yours,

(Signature)
Typed name

1.2.4 The Format of Envelopes

The envelope should match the stationery in color and style. Most companies have the return address in the upper-left corner of the envelope, giving the same information as the letterhead. Otherwise you must type or write your return address the same way as you do for the inside address, usually in smaller typeface than the name and address of the receiver. Name and address of the receiver is always single-spaced with all lines aligned on the left, and they should be in all capital letter, with no punctuation at the end of each line. The order in writing the address is from the smallest division to the largest, just opposite to the Chinese custom in writing addresses.

The in-house notation is placed three lines down the return address and is in all capital letters. The stamp is put at the upper right corner of the envelope with mailing notation, if there are any, given in all capital letters below the stamp.

The format of the address on the envelope can be in blocked or indented style, but it is better to keep the same format with the inside address of the letter.

Skyline Farm Machinery Manufacturing Company
56 Fuan Street, Tianjin, China
Tel.: 0086-22-2236 5566

Stamp

PERSONAL

MS. DAWN ROBERTS
ASIAN FOOD-PROCESSING CO., LTD.
100 KING'S RD
HANOI, VIETNAM

BY AIR

Example 1   (Blocked style)

Linda Smith
12 King's Avenue
Rechmnond
Surrey TW6 ISJ
Britain

Stamp

PERSONAL

MR. GARRY MARSHALL
6345 GLENWOOD DRIVE
ALBUQUERQUE, NM 87001
U.S.A.

PAR AVION

Example 2   (Indented style)

Jack Sill
Central Business Consultants
Hyde Towers
Hong Kong

Stamp

DR. DAWEI ZHANG

NO. 305 JINHUI BUILDING

NANJING RD. HEPING WARD

TIANJIN, CHINA

Example 3　(Mixed style)

1.3　Letters for Example

1.3.1　Letter One

PHILIP TEA EXPORTS LTD.

PO Box 36, Kaduna, Nigeria

Phone: (035) 523471　　Telex:20717　　Our Ref.:VA/ym/48576

June 6, 2018

Plybox Co., Ltd.
PO Box 65, Jacksonville
Florida 32203
For the attention of Mr. Robert Keats

Dear Sirs,

Subject: OVERDUE TEA-CHEST DELIVERY

We wrote to you on June 1 asking for the prompt delivery of our monthly supply of tea chests, which was already 10 days overdue on that date. We have not yet received any delivery or explanation for the delay.

We should appreciate that it is of utmost importance that we are not to let down our customers. If we cannot meet their requirements at the time we agreed upon, we would risk losing them to our competitors.

We ask you, therefore, to deliver our tea chests within a week. Failure to do so will force us to seek quotations urgently from other suppliers.

We sincerely hope that we shall be able to continue doing business with you.

Faithfully yours,

Philip Tea Exports Ltd.
(Signature)
Charles Lai
Managing Director

Enclosure: A copy of our order No.4881

C.C. Michael Konrad
Alicia Montara
Peter D. Schaeffer

1.3.2　Letter Two

Athena House Group
Athena House West Street London SW1Y 2AR
Tel:+44 (0) 20 8302 0261　Fax:+44 (0) 20 8302 4169　E-mail: althena@intl.co.uk
DA/ST

10 May, 2018

Mr. Craig Tomkinson
Manager
Goodison Hotel
42 St Michael's Drive
Leeds
LS1 9EG

Dear sirs,

Will you please send us a copy of catalogue and current price list for garments? We are interested in garments for both men and women, and also for children.

We are one of the leading garment dealers in this city and have branches in eight neighboring towns. If therefore the quality of your garments is satisfactory and the prices are right, we expect to place regular orders for fairly large quantities.

In this case, we should like to know whether you are able to allow us a special discount. This would enable us to maintain the low selling prices that have been an important reason for the growth of our business. In return, we would be prepared to place orders to guarantee annual minimum turn-over, the figure to be mutually agreed.

I look forward to your early reply.

Yours sincerely,
Douglas Allen
Sales Manager

1.3.3   Letter Three

This letter contains the basic parts (blocked letter style).

PHILIP TEA EXPORTS LTD.
PO Box 36, Kaduna, Nigeria
Phone:（035）523471   Telex:20717

10 July, 2018

Mrs. Lorry Mason
National Geographic Society
475 Kenwood St.
Duluth, MN55811
U.S.A.

Dear Mrs. Mason,

Thank you for your letter of 3 July, concerning your forthcoming visit to my company. I'll be glad to meet you at the time of your visit. Please confirm your flight number, so that my assistant,

Helen Wei will be seeing you at the airport.

We look forward to seeing you.

Yours sincerely,

(Signature)
Jenny Chen

1.3.4　Letter Four

This letter contains the basic parts and additional parts (semi-blocked letter style).

==============*TIANJIN TRADE FAIRS*===============
No. 56 Nanjing Rd. Tianjin 300045 China
Tel.:86-22 2366-5783　Fax: 86-22 2366-5758

Our ref.: TF001
Your ref.:

November 20, 2018

CERTIFIED MAIL

Asian Food-processing Equipment Co., Ltd.
100 King's Road
Hanoi, Vietnam

Dear Sirs,

RE: THE FIFTH TIANJIN AGRICULTURAL EQUIPMENT FAIR

The Tianjin Agricultural Equipment Fair will take place from 5 to 13 January, 2018. This fair is an opportunity for both manufacturers and buyers from all over the world to seek business opportunities.

We are now accepting provisional bookings of space. Each year we receive more bookings than we can accommodate. So we advise you to book early if you want to take part in the fair. For representatives from overseas, we are able to arrange visas. (Please provide full passport details.)

Your company would find it worthwhile to have a stand at the fair. Price of the floor space is US $ 150 per sq. m. (min. 15m^2) and payments should be made to a/c 2680805346, Bank of China, Tianjin Branch.

Should you require any further information, please contact us.

Yours faithfully,

TIANJIN TRADE FAIR
(Signature)
Anna Chen, Manager

Enclosure: 10 free VIP tickets to the fair

cc: Eric Long, General Manager

P.S.: You will get 3% discount if you book the space within this month.

1.4   Words and Phrases

1. **routine**   *n.*   the usual or normal way in which you do things   惯例；常规
2. **straightforward**   *adj.*   easy to understand, simple   易懂的；简单的
3. **portray**   *v.*   to represent or describe (someone or something) in a painting, film, book or other artistic work   描绘；描述；描写
4. **approachable**   *adj.*   friendly and easy to talk to   可接近的；平易近人的；亲切的
5. **punctuation**   *n.*   special marks that you add to a text to show the divisions between phrases and sentences, and to make the meaning clearer   标点；标点符号

6. **flimsy**　*adj.*　lacking solidity or strength　易坏的；脆弱的

7. **free from**　解除；没有……的

8. **blemish**　*n.*　a mark on something that spoils its appearance　污点；缺点；瑕疵

9. **clarity**　*n.*　the quality of expressing ideas or thoughts in a clear way　清晰；清楚；明确

10. **ambiguous**　*adj.*　having more than one meaning, so that it is not clear which is intended　歧义的；含糊的；不明确的

11. **conciseness**　*n.*　short and clear, with no unnecessary words　简明

12. **elimination**　*n.*　the removal or destruction of something　排除；除去

13. **wordy**　*adj.*　using too many formal words　多言的；冗长的

14. **jargon**　*n.*　technical words and expressions that are mainly used by people who belong to the same professional group and are difficult to understand　行话

15. **courtesy**　*n.*　polite behavior that shows that you have respect for other people　谦恭；礼貌

16. **redundancy**　*n.*　a situation in which something is not used because something similar or the same already exists　冗余

17. **be bound to**　一定要

18. **diplomacy**　*n.*　the management of relationships between countries, or (fig. approving) skill in dealing with people without making them angry or unhappy, or offending them　外交；交际手段

19. **tact**　*n.*　the ability to be polite and careful about what you say or do so that you do not upset or embarrass other people　得体

20. **in good faith**　诚信的；老实的

21. **stationery**　*n.*　the items needed for writing, such as paper, pens, pencils and envelopes　文具；信纸

1.5　Notes

1. Essentials of Business Letter Writing　商务信函写作的要求（清晰、简洁、礼貌、体谅、正确、具体和完整）

2. The Basic Components of Business Letters 商务信函的基本构成成分

1) **Letterhead**　信头
信头包括公司或集团的名称、地址、电话号码、电传号码、电子邮件地址等。信头一般是印好的。如：

Optical Products Corp.

123 Monmouth Parkway

Long Branch, NJ 07784

Tel: 813-688-1186

Fax: 813-688-112

E-mail: swihgo@welorlalor.net.cn

2) **Date** 日期

日期位于信头的下面，其写法有英式和美式之分。如：

21 March, 2018/21 March 2018（BrE）

January 24, 2018/January 24 2018（AmE）

3) **Inside name and address** 封内名称及地址

封内名称及地址即收信人名称及地址，它与信封上的地址完全相同。设置封内地址的目的在于方便信件的归档、避免差错等。当信封是开窗信封（Window Envelope）时，封内地址还可以当作信封上收件人的地址。封内地址一般位于信头下，它主要包括以下几个要素：

(1) the name of the recipient （收件人姓名）

(2) the department name （部门名称）

(3) company name （公司名称）

(4) suite or room number （房间号或门牌号）

(5) street address （街道名称）

(6) city （城市名称）

(7) postcode （邮编）

(8) state/province and country （州/省和国家名称）

例如：

a.

Mr. James D Keats

General Sales Manager（Import）

W. Brownlaw & Co.

P.O. Box 62, Kirkcaldy

Fife, Scotland

b.

Mrs. George Allen

The Principal

The College of Culture and Language

52 Fruitdale Street

Lowa City, IA 55240-4761

4) **Salutation** 称呼

称呼是写信人对收信人的尊称，多以"Dear"开头，一般位于封内地址或指定收信人姓名的下面两行，通常是从左边顶格写起，在后面加上冒号或逗号。例如：

(1) Dear Sir:/Dear Madam,

(2) Dear Sirs:/ Dear Mesdames:

(3) Dear Mr. Smith:/Dear Ms. Alexander:/Dear Mrs. Donovan:/Dear Miss Essiet:

(4) Dear Felix Bryan:

5) **Body**　正文

正文是信函最重要的一部分，表达了写信人的观点、意见、目的、愿望等。正文通常位于称呼下一行或两行位置处，行与行之间设置单倍行距，段落与段落之间设置双倍行距。通常情况下，正文由三部分构成。第一部分是开头语（Opening Sentence），习惯上开头语是写信人对收信日期、编号、简要内容等做简要叙述，使对方立即知道此信是针对哪封信而写的；如果是首次信函联系，则利用开头语做简单的自我介绍，简明扼要地表明写此信的意图。开头语一般自成一段。第二部分为信函内容。最后一部分是结束语（Closing Sentence），用以总结信中所谈及的事项，对收信人提出希望和要求，其位置是在正文之后另起一段。

6) **Complimentary Close**　结束敬语

与称呼一样，结束敬语是表示写信人的一种谦称，以较礼貌的方式结束信函。结束敬语位于正文后一行或两行处，首字母需大写，后面加上逗号。每封信的结束敬语必须与开头的称呼相匹配，以反映发信人与收信人的关系。常用的结束敬语如下表所示。

最正式的（一般用于对上级的回信）	Respectfully, Respectfully yours, Yours respectfully, Very respectfully
正式的	Yours truly, Very truly yours, Yours faithfully, Faithfully yours
普通式的（对方来信时多以名字来称呼）	Yours sincerely, Sincerely yours, Very sincerely yours
简略式的（表示亲密）	Cordially yours, Cordially

7) **Signature**　签名

签名包括亲笔签名和打印签名，位于结束敬语下方。签名是商务信函中极为重要的部分，因为签名具有一定的法律效力。签名者对信中所叙述的内容承担一定的责任，因而签名要清晰可辨，独具风格。签名可用全签署，如：James Adolf；也可用简略签署，即姓名用全称，其余部分则取其第一个字母，如：J. Adolf。如果写信人是代表公司，则要将公司的名称打印在签名之前；如果写信人不在场，可让秘书或其他人代签，在姓名前面加上 P.P.（Per Procurationem）或 For；如果写信人是女性，则可在签名的后面加上 Miss，Mrs.，Ms. 等。此外，由于签名往往潦草而不易识别，在签名下面一行必须将签署的姓名打印出来。如果写信人有职位，也应在其姓名下打印出来。

3. Additional Components of Business Letters 商务信函的其他成分

1) **Mailing or In-house Notation**　邮递方式

邮递方式位于日期下方两行处且以大写字母表示。

2) **Reference**　编号

编号是便于参考查阅之用的，通常位于信头下方。它包括卷宗号、部门代码、主办人（寄信人和打字人）姓名的首写字母。

3) **Attention Line**　主送，简写为 Attn.。

当发信人希望直接将此信发给特定的人或部门处理而且又知晓其姓名或部门名称时可

以使用主送，通常在封内地址及称呼之间或在封内地址内且在缩行式正文上方中心处写上收件人或部门。例如：

(1) Attention: Mr.John P. Rogers, President

(2) For the attention of Mr. James P. Dahl

(3) Attention: Personnel Department

(4) Attention of Sales & Marketing Department

(5) For the attention: Miss Wang Ying

4) **Subject Line/Caption**　标题或事由

标题或事由概括了信函大意，位于称呼及正文之间，通常在称呼下方两行处，以便引起收信人注意，使其立即知道信件的主旨，也有利于归档、查阅。事由要简洁，说明商品的名称、数量、合同号、信用证号等即可。

5) **Multiple-Page Letter Heading**　多页信的标题

当信函不止一页时，在首页注明信头，其后的各页纸张应该同第一页具有相同的质量、大小和颜色。多页信的标题应有收信人名称或其所在机构、页码和日期。

6) **Reference Initials**　主办人代号

主办人代号位于左边，签名下面空两行或三行处，作用是便于双方了解关于某事的主办人和打印此信人的姓名。

7) **Enclosure Notation**　附件

附件位于主办人代号下面空两行处。如果附件不止一个，应注明 2 Encls.或 3 Encls.等，或者详细列明具体的附件。例如：

Enc.:　1 quality certificate　（一份质量证明）

　　　　2 commercial invoices　（两张商业发票）

　　　　1 B/L　（一张海运提单）

　　　　1 packing list（一张装箱单）

8) **Carbon Copy Notation**　抄送

如果写信人将此信抄送给其他个人或团体，同时让收信人知道此信抄送给哪些人或团体，那么就在信末左下角注明"C.C."或"c.c."字样，随后写上有关人员或团体的名字。如果副本寄给两个或两个以上的人，就按姓名的字母顺序来排列。例如：

(1) C.C.：Peter D. Schaeffer

(2) c.c.：Group Personnel and Training Manager, BHL

　　　　　The Senior Training Office, BHL

bcc 的意思是"密抄送"。当发信人不希望其他人知道某人过目某封信时，可以使用 bcc 将信中密抄送某人。抄送直接位于附件或主办人代号下方。

9) **Postscript/P.S.**　附言

若写信人在信的正文中忘了写而又想补充某事时，常常在 P.S.后加上想补充的内容，放在抄送下方空两行处。例如：

P. S. The sample will be forwarded under separate cover next Friday.

在商务信函中，一般不用附言；但在私人信函中，附言会较为频繁地使用。尽管附言能够起到强调的效果，但是在较为正式的商务信函中应尽量避免使用，因为使用附言会显得写信人办事不够周密。

4. Formats of a Business Letter 商务信函的格式

商务信函有不同的格式，选用什么样的格式因人而异。不过有些公司的所有信函都采取统一格式，以体现公司的独特风格。常见的商务信函格式包括以下三种。

1) **Blocked Format** 平头式或全齐头式

在平头式（全齐头式）商务信函中，所有信行都是从左边界开始，并且整封信中均无行首缩格。这种格式简单，易于打印，是商务信函中最常采用的一种格式。

2) **Semi-blocked Format** 半齐头式

在半齐头式商务信函中，日期、信尾敬语和签名是从纸张中线偏右处开始打印的，其他的要素均从左边界开始。这是一种比较保守的格式。

3) **Indented Format** 缩行式

在缩行式商务信函中，信的正文中每一行通常都要缩进 4~5 个空格，其他要素的位置与半齐头式的位置相同。

1.6　Useful Expressions

1. We wrote to you on 15 January asking for the prompt delivery of our monthly supply of tea chests, which was already 10 days overdue on that date.

我们 1 月 15 日写信给你们，要求按月向我方供应的茶叶箱迅速装运，这已经比约定日期迟到 10 天了。

2. We should appreciate that it is of utmost importance that we are not to let down our customers.

我们应意识到不让顾客失望是非常重要的。

3. Failure to do so will force us to seek quotations urgently from other suppliers.

未能做到这些将迫使我们紧急向其他供应商寻求报价。

4. We are one of the leading garment dealers in this city and have branches in eight neighboring towns.

我们是该城市的最主要的服装经销商之一，并且在八个邻近市镇设有分支机构。

5. If therefore the quality of your garments is satisfactory and the prices are right, we expect to place regular orders for fairly large quantities.

如果贵方服装质量令人满意，价格合理，我们将大量地进行常规订购。

6. This fair is an opportunity for both manufacturers and buyers from all over the world to seek business opportunities.

此次展销会为那些来自世界各地的寻求商业合作的制造商和买主提供了机会。

1.7　Exercises

1. Answer the following questions.

(1) What are the 7 Cs when people talk about the certain essential qualities of business letters?

(2) What are the basic components and additional components of business letters?

(3) What are the three letter formats?

2. Choose the best answer to complete the following statements.

(1) A letterhead includes _____.

A. name of the company　　　　　　　　B. the E-mail address

C. address of the company　　　　　　　D. all of above

(2) The inside address contains all of the following information, except _____.

A. company name　　　　　　　　　　　B. the date of typing of the message

C. the name of the city and the country　D. the name of the state

(3) For a multiple-page letter, _____ should only be used on the first page.

A. letterhead　　　　　　　　　　　　　B. paper of the same quality

C. paper of the same size　　　　　　　　D. paper of the same quality

(4) A mail notation should be included in which of the following cases: _____.

A. the exact address is unknown

B. the sender has something exciting mentioned in the letter

C. the letter is confidential and only readable to someone intended

D. none of the above

(5) What does the subject line tell the recipients?

A. What the letter is about.　　　　　　　B. When the letter has been sent.

C. Who wrote the letter.　　　　　　　　D. Who typed the letter.

3. Arrange the following in the proper form as they should be set out in a letter.

(1) Sender's name: China National Light Industrial Products Import & Export Corporation, Shanghai Branch

(2) Sender's address: 123 Jiefang Road, Shanghai, China

(3) Sender's Fax Number: 86-22-67891236

(4) Sender's e-mail address: linda@mail. zlnet. com. cn

(5) Date: March 18, 2018

(6) Receiver's name: H. G. Wilkinson Company Limited

(7) Receiver's address: 456 Lombart Street, Lagos Nigeria

(8) Salutation used: Dear Sirs

(9) Subject Line: Sewing Machines

(10) The message:

① We thank you for your letter of March 6 inquiring for the captioned goods.

② The enclosed booklet contains details of all our Sewing Machines and will enable you to make a suitable selection.

③ We look forward to receiving your specific inquiry with keen interest.

(11) Complimentary close used: Yours faithfully,

4. Address an envelope to the above letter.

Answers for Reference

Chapter 2　Establishing Business Relations

2.1　Introduction

Today, a global market place is emerging. Most nations have become more and more dependent on each other and business relations play the important role in international trade. Therefore, it is essential that business relations are established.

Now, it is fairly true to say no customer, no business. In order to enlarge market share and promote sales, companies have to establish relations with new customers besides keeping existing ones. And to establish business relations with prospective dealers is one of the vitally important measures either for a newly established firm or an old one that wishes to enlarge its business scope and turnover.

In trade, suppliers and buyers are usually in search of each other before transaction, and establishing business relations is the first step of trade and development. The following are the major sources where information about potential customers is available:

(1) the banks;

(2) the periodicals;

(3) the advertisements;

(4) the introduction from your business connections and friends;

(5) directories of importers and exporters;

(6) business houses of the same trade;

(7) the market investigation;

(8) the Commercial Counselor's Office;

(9) the Chambers of Commerce both at home and abroad;

(10) self-introduction by merchants themselves;

(11) Internet.

Of all the above sources, information from your business connections and friends, the Chambers of Commerce both at home and abroad and the Commercial Counselor's Office is usually more reliable but is subject to certain fees and charges.

In choosing a customer or partner in foreign countries, some researches are often needed to have a better knowledge about the country or region in such aspects as:

(1) business policy and customs practice;

(2) political and economic stability;

(3) diplomatic relation with your own country;

(4) culture and interests of potential buyers;

(5) geographic conditions (such as ports, shipping lines);

(6) natural environment (such as climate).

Besides extending your desire to target companies to establish business relations, you may introduce your own company and products to the public through appropriate media, such as website, brochure to solicit business and attract potential customers and partners.

When we need to establish business relations with the merchants abroad, we can approach them through some of the following channels:

(1) communication in writing (e-mails, faxes, letters, etc.);

(2) attendance at the export commodities fairs;

(3) contact at exhibitions held at home or abroad;

(4) mutual visits by trade delegations and groups.

Of all these channels, the first one is most constantly used in business activities.

The first letter to open up a market or enlarge your firm business scope is very important, because it is known that first impression will count heavily. Therefore, transaction can only be made after the business connections have been set up. Establishing business relations involve not only language communication skills but also some practical business negotiation techniques, particularly when trying to go into business relations with new potential customers.

2.2 Writing Guide

Having obtained the desired names and addresses of the firms from any of the sources, you may start sending letters to parties concerned. Generally speaking, when writing such a letter for building up business relations, you should inform the recipient of the following:

(1) the source from which you get the information.

(2) your intention in writing.

(3) your business and main scope of products. If there are any detailed product catalogues and relevant information, include them as attachment or enclosure or refer your readers to your website. If you intend to buy for import, you may also make a request for samples, price lists, catalogues, etc.

(4) the reference as to your firm's financial position and integrity (if possible).

(5) your expectation of cooperation and receiving an early reply from the recipient.

This type of letter is an outgoing letter and may be called a "first inquiry". Generally, this letter consists of three major parts: opening, body and closing. The opening paragraph includes the source from which you get the information and your intention in writing. The body of the letter includes your business and main scope of products, the reference as to your firm's financial position and integrity (if possible) and so on. The closing paragraph includes your expectation of cooperation and receiving an early reply from the recipient.

Letters for establishing business relations often involve introduction of the firm. When giving such introductions, you should make it brief and focus on information most attractive and important to your recipient. Leave long and not very important details in your company's website or introductory brochures. Sometimes, you may use superlative degree of adjectives such as "best", "largest" sparingly, as they may sound bragging and boasting. If you must use these words, support them with facts and figures.

Be sure to answer a letter of such kind without any delay after we receive it and with courtesy so as to create goodwill and leave a good impression on the reader. This will lay the foundations for the transaction in future. In reply to letters, you should:

(1) mention the date in which you have received the letter;

(2) express your thanks to your reader for the proposal;

(3) provide information requested;

(4) state clearly whether you accept the proposal or not;

(5) give a reason if you decline it, and end your letter with a positive note for future business.

2.3　Letters for Example

2.3.1　An introduction of an Exporter

SOUTH CHINA SILK PRODUCT CO., LTD.

Nanjing, China

Tel: 86-022 43567788

July 15, 2018

Universal Channel Corp.

5 Rock Street

Rockbridge, IL62081

U.S.A.

Dear Sirs,

We owe your name and address to the Commercial Counselor's Office of the American Embassy in Beijing who has informed us that you are in the market for silk product. We avail ourselves of this opportunity to approach you for the establishment of trade relations with you.

South China Silk Product Co., Ltd. is one of the leading manufacturers of silk products in China, with the headquarter based in Nanjing, China. The company enjoys excellent reputation through 32 years of business experience in this field. Its products range from the traditional embroidered silk blouse to the latest fashion, some of which have been displayed in the latest fashion show in Paris, and are well received by customers at home and abroad. They even attracted many celebrities and dignitaries including the former British Prime Minister Madam Thatcher.

We have a reliable and committed work team of 2,000 employees. In our business practice, we strive for a win-win result with our customers based on the principle of equality and mutual benefits. So we are sure that you will be quite satisfied with our services and the excellent quality of our goods. For further details about our company and our products, please visit our website at www.scspc.com. Concerning our financial status and reputation, please direct all inquiries to the Bank of China, Nanjing Branch. Should any of the items be of interest to you, please let us know. We shall be glad to give you our the lowest quotations upon receipt of your detailed requirements. It is our hope to promote, by joint efforts, both trade and friendship to our mutual advantages.

Thank you very much for your co-operation. You are cordially invited to visit our company at your convenience and we look forward to receiving your favorable reply.

Sincerely yours,

SOUTH CHINA SILK PRODUCT CO. ,LTD.

(Signature)

Larry Chang, Director

2.3.2　A Positive Reply from an Importer

Universal Channel Corp.

5 Rock Street, Rockbridge, IL #62081

Tel: 858-8905-3366

July 22, 2018

Mr. LARRY CHANG

South China Silk Product Co., Ltd.

31 Hubei Rd.

Nanjing, China

Dear Mr. Larry Chang,

We thank you for your letter of July 15, 2018 and shall be glad to enter into business relations with you for the sale of silk products.

I believe a friendly trade relation will benefit both sides. Presently we are interested in Art. No.36 displayed on your website. Please send us your samples and price list, as well as information about terms of payment and time of delivery.

Your prompt reply is highly appreciated.

Sincerely,

(Signature)

Renee Easton

2.3.3 A Negative Reply from an Importer

Universal Channel Corp.

5 Rock Street, Rockbridge, IL #62081

Tel: 858-8905-3366

July 22, 2018

Mr. LARRY CHANG

South China Silk Product Co., Ltd.

31 Hubei Rd.

Nanjing, China

Dear Mr. Larry Chang,

   Thank you for your letter of July 15, 2018 introducing your company and informing us of the business opportunity.

   Presently, our orders for the first half of the year have already been filled.

   However, we will contact you when we need to place an order.

Sincerely,

(Signature)

Renee Easton

2.3.4 An Introduction of an Importer

Universal Channel Corp.

5 Rock Street, Rockbridge, IL #62081

Tel: 858-8905-3366

July 15, 2018

South China Silk Product Co., Ltd.
15 Fujian Rd.
Beijing, China

Dear Sirs,

We learn from China Business Directory that you are one of the leading exporters of silk products in your country. We take this opportunity to approach you in the hope of establishing business relations with you.

We are an important dealer in silk products, having many years of experience in this line of business and believe that there is a promising market in our country for your products.

Please send us your catalogue and price list at your earliest convenience.

Yours faithfully,

(Signature)
Renee Aston

2.3.5　A Reply from an Exporter on Transferring Business Relations

SOUTH CHINA SILK PRODUCT CO., LTD.

Nanjing, China

Tel: 86-022 43567788

July 22, 2018

Universal Channel Corp.

5 Rock Street

Abridge, IL62081

U.S.A.

Dear Sirs,

Re: embroidered silk handkerchief

Your letter of July 15, 2018 addressed to our Beijing Branch Office has been passed on to us for attention and reply, as the captioned goods come under the scope of our trade activities.

We are regretful to inform you that the product you required has already been transferred to Thailand. And it has been represented by South China Silk Product Co., (Thailand) Ltd., 226 Davis Street, Bangkok, Thailand. As a result, we are no longer in a position to make you an offer for it but would rather recommend that you approach them directly for your requirements.

Should any other items be of interest to you, please do not hesitate to contact us. It is our pleasure to offer you at any time.

Yours faithfully,

South China Silk Product Co., (China) Ltd.

Tony Li, Sales Manager

2.3.6　Letter Referring to the Reference

Dear Sirs,

Your name has been given to us as a credit reference by South China Silk Product Co., Ltd., who wants to start business with us. We should be highly obliged if you could let us have your opinion on their reputation and their financial standing.

Any information you may provide us will be treated in strict confidence.

Yours faithfully,

(Signature)

Renee Easton

2.4　Words and Phrases

1. **prospective**　*adj.*　likely to do a particular thing or achieve a particular position　预期的；可能的；未来的

2. **dealer**　*n.*　someone who buys and sells a particular product　经销商；商人

3. **vitally**　*adv.*　extremely important and necessary for something to succeed or exist　极其重要的；必不可少的

4. **turnover**　*n.*　the amount of business done in a period of time　（一定时期的）营业额；成交量；交易额

5. **available**　*adj.*　able to be obtained, used, or reached　可用的；可得到的；可达到的

6. **periodical**　*n.*　a magazine or newspaper, esp. on a serious subject, that is published regularly　期刊

7. **reliable**　*adj.*　someone or something can be trusted or depended on　可信赖的；可靠的

8. **diplomatic**　*adj.*　concerning or involving the work of diplomats　外交的

9. **appropriate**　*adj.*　correct or suitable for a particular time, situation, or purpose　恰当的；合适的

10. **brochure**　*n.*　a thin book giving information or advertising something　小册子

11. **solicit**　*v.*　to sell something by taking orders for a products or service　招揽（生意）

12. **mutual**　*adj.*　（of two or more people or groups）feeling the same emotion, or doing the same thing to or for each other　相互的；彼此的

13. **delegation**　*n.*　a group of people who represent a company, organization, etc.　代表团

14. **involve**　*v.*　to include something as a necessary part or result　包含（必要的部分或结果）；包括；需要

15. **superlative degree**　最高级

16. **brag**　*v.*　to talk too proudly about what you have done, what you own, etc.　自夸；吹嘘

17. **boast**　*v.*　to talk too proudly about your abilities, achievements, or possessions because you want to make other people admire you　夸口；夸耀；吹嘘

18. **goodwill**　*n.*　the success of a company, and its good relationship with its customers, calculated as part of its value when it is sold　商誉；信誉

19. **foundations** *n.* the solid layer of cement, bricks, stones, etc., that is under a building to support it 地基；基础

20. **proposal** *n.* a plan or suggestion which is made formally to an official person or group, or the act of making it 计划；建议；提议；计划或建议的提出

21. **celebrity** *n.* a famous person 名人

22. **dignitary** *n.* a person of high rank or position 高官

23. **committed** *adj.* willing to work very hard at something 乐于献身的；尽责的

24. **strive for** 奋斗；争取

25. **convenience** *n.* what is easiest and best for a particular person （个人的）便利；自在；舒适

26. **prompt** *adj.* done quickly, immediately, or at the right time 迅速的；立刻的；及时的

27. **embroider** *v.* to make a pattern of stitches on cloth with colored cotton or silk threads 刺绣；绣花；在……上刺绣

28. **transfer** *v.* to move something from one place or position to another 搬运；转移；前移

29. **recommend** *v.* to praise something or someone, or suggest them for a particular purpose or job 推荐；介绍

30. **hesitate** *v.* to pause before saying or doing something because you are not sure or nervous 犹豫；踌躇；迟疑（不决）

2.5 Notes

1. **Commercial Counselor's Office** 商务参赞处

2. **Chambers of Commerce both at home and abroad** 国内外商会

3. **open up** 开发

4. **build up** 建立

5. **financial position** 财务状况

6. **without any delay** 赶快；立刻；毫不迟延

7. **lay the foundations** 打地基

8. **owe one's name and address to** 承蒙……告知贵公司的名称和地址
类似的表达方式有：
Through the courtesy of …, we come to know your name and address.
We are indebted to … for your name and address.

9. **be in the market for** 想要购买

e.g.　One of our customers is in the market for Chinese Black Tea.
　　　我方一位客户想要购买中国红茶。

10. **avail oneself of** 利用

e.g. We avail ourselves of this opportunity to write to you and see if we can establish business relations with you.

我们利用此次机会写信给贵方，看看是否能够与贵方建立贸易关系。

11. **approach** *v.* 接洽；与……接洽（和 contact 同义，但被动语态用 approach 较多）

e.g. Please approach (contact) them again.

请再次与他们联系。

We have been approached by several buyers for the supply of sesames.

有好几家买主与我方接洽购买芝麻。

12. **leading** *adj.* 最主要的

e.g. leading importer   主要进口商

leading market   主要市场

leading stock   主要股份

13. **enjoy excellent reputation** 享有盛誉

类似的表达方式有：enjoy great popularity/be most popular with…/enjoy fast sales/be universally acknowledged

e.g. The goods have enjoyed great popularity in world market.

产品已在世界市场上享有盛誉。

The goods are most popular with our customers.

产品非常受我们的顾客欢迎。

The goods have commanded a good market.

产品畅销。

The goods are selling fast (or enjoy fast sales).

产品畅销。

The goods are universally acknowledged.

产品被普遍认可。

14. **mutual benefits**   互利互惠

15. **by joint efforts**   共同努力

类似表达方式有：through/by joint/mutual/collective efforts

16. **favorable** *adj.* 有利的；赞成的；有帮助的

favorable reply   合意的回答，类似 good news，相当于中文的"佳音""好消息"

favorable price   优惠价格

表示赞同某事或表示对某人、某事有利，后接介词 to

e.g. We are favorable to your terms and conditions of this transaction.

我们同意你方这个交易的条件。

The market has so changed as to be favorable to the sellers.

市场变为对卖方有利。

如果表示对某种行为有利一般接介词 for

e.g.　The time is not favorable for the disposal of the goods.
　　　现在不是卖货的有利时机。

17. enter into business relations with　与……建立贸易联系

类似的表达方式有：enter into trade relations/relationship with/establish business relations with

e.g.　We are writing with a desire to enter into direct business relations with you.
　　　为了与贵公司建立贸易关系，特致函联系。

18. terms of payment　支付方式；付款条件

19. time of delivery　装船期；交货期

20. appreciate　*v.*　感谢；感激（可接动名词，不可接不定式）；理解；体会

e.g.　We highly appreciate your kind cooperation.
　　　我们十分感激你方的合作。

　　　We shall appreciate your giving this matter your serious consideration.
　　　如贵方对此事认真考虑，我们将不胜感激。

　　　We shall appreciate it if you will send us a brochure and sample book by air immediately.
　　　如能立即航寄一份说明书和一份样本，不胜感激。

　　　We hope you will appreciate our position.
　　　希望贵方能理解我们的处境。

　　　It will be greatly appreciated if you will send us your samples immediately.
　　　如能立即寄来你方样品，我们将不胜感激。

　　　Your prompt reply will be greatly appreciated.
　　　如能尽快回复，将不胜感激。

21. contact　*v.*　与……联系；与……接触
　　　　　n.　联系；交往

e.g.　For further details, please contact our local office.
　　　详情请向我们当地的分支机构探询。

　　　We have been in contact with that firm for nearly two years.
　　　我们与那家公司有近两年的交往。

22. place an order　订货

place an order for sth. with sb.　向某人订购某物

e.g.　If your price is competitive, we shall be glad to place an order for Black Tea with your company.
　　　如果你方产品的价格具有竞争力，我们会向贵公司订购红茶。

23. Business Directory　企业名录

24. catalogue　*n.*　目录（也可以写作 catalog)

latest catalogue　最新目录

25. **standing**　*n.*　资信情况；信誉

　　　　　　　adj.　固定的；永久的

e.g.　standing cost　长期成本；固定成本

　　　standing orders　长期订单

　　　standing director　常务董事

26. **We are permitted to mention the Bank of America, Washington, as a reference**.

我们已征得华盛顿的美国银行同意，把它作为我们的咨询银行。

27. **come under the scope of our trade activities**　属于经营范围

类似的表达方式有：be/lie within the scope of one's trade activities 或 be/lie/fall within one's

business scope

28. **be in a position to**　能够（指处于能够做某事的地位）

2.6　Useful Expressions

1. 告知信息来源

(1) We owe your name and address to the Chamber of Commerce in your country who has informed us that you are in the market for silk product.

承蒙贵国商会的介绍，我们得知贵公司想要购买丝绸制品。

(2) We have obtained your name and address through the Bank of China and understood that you would like to establish business relations with us.

我公司从中国银行得到贵公司的名称和地址，并获悉贵公司愿同我方建立业务关系。

(3) We have obtained your address in the China Business Directory.

我们从中国企业名录获得你方地址。

(4) We learned from the Chinese Chamber of Commerce here that you are producing silk products.

我们从这里的中国商会得知，贵方生产丝绸制品。

(5) We got the information from our sales manager that you have the desire to cooperate with our firm in marketing our silk products.

我方从我们的销售经理处得知，贵方愿与我公司合作营销我们的丝绸制品。

(6) Your company has kindly been introduced to us by Messrs. Freeman & Co., Ltd., London, England. We shall be pleased to enter into business relations with you at an early date.

英国伦敦的弗里曼股份有限公司向我们介绍了贵公司。我们很高兴能早日与贵方建立业务关系。

2. 表示建立业务关系的愿望

(1) We avail ourselves of this opportunity to approach you for the establishment of trade relations with you.

我们利用此次机会与贵方接洽，以期与贵方建立业务关系。

(2) We are writing to you in the hope that we can open up business relations with your firm.

我们写信给贵方，希望我们能够与贵方开始业务关系。

(3) In order to extend our export business to your country, we wish to enter into direct business relations with you.

为了扩大我们在贵国的出口业务，我们希望与贵方建立直接的业务关系。

(4) We wish to express our desire to trade with you in silk products.

我们想要表达我们在丝制产品上同贵方做贸易的愿望。

3. 自我介绍

(1) Our company is one of the leading manufacturers of silk products in China, with the headquarter based in Nanjing, China.

我公司是中国丝绸制品的主要生产商之一，总部设在中国南京。

(2) We wish to introduce ourselves to you as a state-owned corporation dealing exclusively in silk products.

兹介绍，我公司是一家专营丝绸制品的国有公司。

(3) Our corporation is a group enterprise integrating scientific research, business, production and service. As a joint venture, our corporation has won a prominent position in the field of silk products in China.

我们公司是一家集科研、商贸、生产和服务于一体的企业集团。作为一家合资企业，我们公司已经在中国丝绸制品领域赢得显著地位。

(4) We inform you that we have been engaged in this business for the past 25 years. We, therefore, feel that because of our past years' experience, we are well qualified to take care of your interests at this end.

请知晓我公司已从事此项业务 25 年，因此，我们认为凭借我们历年的经验，我方完全有能力在该领域照顾好贵方利益。

(5) As for ourselves, we are a leading and old established firm of exporters, and we are in a very good position to supply most grades of silk products at competitive prices and for good delivery.

我们是一家最主要的老字号出口企业，能够以有竞争力的价格和良好的交货期提供大多数等级的丝绸制品。

4. 业务范围介绍

(1) Silk products fall (come) within the scope of our business activities.
丝绸制品在我们的业务范围之内。

(2) Silk products are our line.
丝绸制品是我们的经营业务。

(3) The main products our corporation deals in are silk products.

我们公司经营的主要产品是丝绸制品。

(4) Our corporation is established for the purpose of carrying on import and export business as well as other activities in connection with foreign trade.

我们公司的建立旨在开展与外贸相关的进出口业务和其他活动。

(5) We are in a position to accept orders against customers' samples specifying design, specifications and packaging requirements. We are also prepared to accept orders for goods with customers' own trademarks or brand names.

我们能够接受按照顾客样品指定的设计、规格和包装要求的订单。我们也准备接受客户自有商标或品牌的商品订单。

5. 索取资料或样品

(1) Please send us your samples and price list, as well as information about terms of payment and time of delivery.

请将贵方样品和价格单以及有关支付方式和交货期的资料寄予我方。

(2) We invite you to send us details and prices, possibly also samples, of such goods that you would be interested in selling, and we shall gladly study the sales possibilities in our market.

我们邀请贵方将你方希望销售的商品的详细资料和价格发送给我们，如果可以的话请将样品也发送给我们，我们将很高兴地研究其在我方市场上销售的可能性。

(3) We shall thank you to let us know your trade terms, and forward samples and other helpful literature, with a view to getting into business in the near future.

考虑到在不久的将来与贵方建立业务关系，如果贵方让我们知晓贵方贸易条款并将样本和其他有用的商品说明书之类的印刷品寄交我们，我方将不胜感激。

(4) If you can supply this type of merchandise, kindly airmail us a sample cup. Also, please enclose your price list and all suitable illustrations.

如果贵方能够供应此类商品，请将样杯空邮给我们。另外，请将贵方价格单和所有与之相匹配的说明一同寄来。

6. 随函附寄

(1) We look forward to receiving your order and meanwhile enclose a copy of our catalogue as we feel you may be interested in some of our other products.

我们盼望收到贵方订单，同时随函附上一份我们认为贵方感兴趣的我方其他产品的目录。

(2) We enclose herewith a list of goods to supply you from prime sources at the lowest possible prices.

我们在此装入一份来自出产地的最低价格的商品目录供你方参考。

(3) To give you a general idea of the silk products now available for export, we enclose a brochure and a price list. Quotations and sample books will be airmailed to you upon receipt of your specific inquiry.

　　为了让贵方对我方现在可供出口的丝绸制品有一般性的了解，我们随函附上一个小册子和一张价格单。我们在收到贵方具体询盘后会将报价单和样本簿以航空邮件形式寄给贵方。

　　(4) In order to give you a rough idea of our various silk products, we are airmailing you under separate cover a copy of our latest catalogue for your reference. If you find any of the items interesting, please let us know as soon as possible. We shall be glad to send you quotations and samples upon receipt of your concrete inquiries.

　　为了让贵方对我方各式各样的丝绸制品有个大致的了解，我们以航空邮件形式另邮了一份我们最近的目录供贵方参考。如果贵方对任何一项商品感兴趣，请尽快让我们知晓。在收到贵方具体的询盘后，我们非常乐意将报价单和样本寄给贵方。

7．结尾句

(1) We look forward to receiving your favorable reply.
我方期待您的佳音。

(2) Your prompt reply is highly appreciated.
如能尽快回复，将不胜感激。

(3) We will contact you when we need to place an order.
当我们需要下订单时将与贵方联系。

2.7　Exercises

1. Translate the terms and expressions from Chinese into English.

（1）商务参赞处　　　　　　（2）财务状况

（3）毫不迟延　　　　　　　（4）建立业务关系

（5）在某人方便的时候　　　（6）售后服务

（7）互利互惠　　　　　　　（8）属于……的经营范围

2. Fill in the blanks with appropriate words.

(1) We are _____ to _____ that you are one of the leading textile exporters in U.S.A.

(2) We _____ your name and address _____ your Commerce Counselor's Office.

(3) Should any items be _____ interest to you, please let us know.

(4) We _____ this opportunity to approach you for the establishment of trade relations with you.

(5) As the item _____ the scope of our business activities, we shall be pleased to establish direct trade relations with you.

(6) We take _____ _____ _____ writing to you in the hope of entering into business relations with you.

(7) _____ receipt of your _____ inquiry, we shall send you immediately our quotation sheet.

(8) If your price is _____ , we shall place an trial order _____ you _____ your new products.

3. Fill in the blanks with the words and phrases given below, and change the form when necessary.

offer	under	upon receipt of	enter	through	know
enjoy	acquaint	in the market for	learn	fall/come	effort

We ___(1)___ from the Chamber of Commerce that you are ___(2)___ silk products. Since this article ___(3)___ within the scope of our business activities, we take this opportunity to express our wish to ___(4)___ into business relations with you.

Good Luck brand silk products are ___(5)___ for their good quality and fine workmanship. They have enjoyed great popularity in the U.S. market. We are sure that ___(6)___ our joint ___(7)___ they will ___(8)___ fast sale in your market.

In order to ___(9)___ you with our products, we are airmailing to you ___(10)___ separate cover several brochures together with a price list. ___(11)___ your specific inquiry, we shall send you our ___(12)___ without delay.

4. Translate the following Sentences into Chinese.

(1) We wish to extend our warm welcome to your desire to enter into direct business relations with us in the line of silk products.

(2) We write to introduce ourselves as exporters of silk handkerchief having many years of experience in this particular line of business.

(3) We are given to understand that you are potential buyers of Chinese silk products, which comes within the scope of our business activities.

(4) We wish to introduce ourselves to you as a state-owned import and export corporation dealing in silk products.

(5) Your company has been recommended to us through the courtesy of the Chamber of Commerce in your country.

(6) We shall be obliged if you would send us samples and prices of your products.

(7) To acquaint you with the products we handle, we are sending you under cover several sample books.

(8) Our products are sold in many countries and enjoy good reputation in the world market.

(9) Please submit full specifications of your refrigerators together with terms of payment and discount rate.

(10) We are looking forward to your favorable reply.

5. Translate the following Sentences into English.

（1）你方七月十八日希望同我方建立业务关系的信已经收到，谢谢。

（2）承蒙弗里曼公司介绍，得悉你公司是贵国丝制产品最大的进口商之一。

（3）作为英国主要的进口商之一，我们此次写信给贵公司是希望与贵公司建立直接贸易关系。

（4）据了解，贵公司是中国丝绸制品有潜力的买主，而该商品正属于我方的业务经营范围。

（5）我们利用此机会致函贵方以了解可否与贵方建立贸易关系。

（6）我们的产品驰名中外、久享盛誉，相信在贵国有很大的市场潜力。

（7）如果贵方需要更多有关我方业务状况的信息，我们乐意随时给予答复。

（8）请告知你方的具体需要，以便我公司另寄目录及报价单。

（9）我们盼望早日得到你方的答复并相信通过相互合作，我们不久即可达成这笔交易。

（10）承蒙巴黎商会告知贵公司名称和地址，并得知贵公司是桌布进口商。

6. Translate the following letter into English.

敬启者：

承蒙美国商会告知贵公司名称和地址，并得知贵公司想要进口中国生产的电器用品。我公司是生产所附目录中的电器用品的制造商，希望贵公司对这些产品感兴趣。

如贵公司需要进一步了解有关我们公司或有关产品的情况，请随时与我们联系。

盼即复。

Answers for Reference

Chapter 3   Inquires

3.1   Introduction

People often need information about prices, products, services that other company can supply. They may require a quotation or an estimate for products. An inquiry is such a request for information about certain commodity or service and the trade terms as well. It is often made by buyers to sellers and usually the first step of a business transaction. Therefore, writing of inquiries has become the usual practice of business correspondence.

In a routine letter of inquiry, a buyer will state clearly and concisely the general information he wants, including a catalogue, a price list, a sample, a quotation, an estimate and so on. As far as the content is concerned, inquiries are of two types: general and specific. The former is sent to acquire some general information about products, such as asking for price lists, samples, catalogues and terms of payment. The latter expresses a definite wish to purchase a specific product if conditions are met, and it requires more detailed information such as price terms, quantity, port of shipment, and packing.

A "first inquiry", that is an inquiry sent to a supplier with whom we have not yet done business, should begin by telling the supplier how we obtained his name. Some details of our own business, such as the kind of goods handled, quantities needed, usual terms of trading, and any information which are likely to enable the supplier to decide what he can do for us, will also help.

An inquiry should be written directly and clearly. And an inquiry must be acknowledged by way of establishing goodwill. Because it could lead to important business. If it is from an old customer, say how you appreciate it; if it is from a new customer, say you are glad to receive it and express the hope of a lasting and friendly business relationship. Nowadays, many firms even use a printed inquiry form instead of a letter. We need only to fill in the form with the necessary information. Some companies provide an online inquiry system that enables us to send our inquiries easily and quickly.

In the reply to inquiry, all inquiries should be replied promptly. Our response and the time it takes us to reply are critical to be successful. Reply today with complete information for best results. A reply should answer all the questions mentioned in inquiry. If samples are needed by the inquirer or his/her company, we should send the samples as soon as possible. Of course, we may ask our receiver to share the cost by paying the postage, because sometimes sample cost is also a very heavy burden.

3.2　Writing Guide

　　When writing an inquiry, we should address directly to the person in charge, in this way, our letter will receive immediate attention. And we may give the name of the product in the subject line so that our reader will get the main idea of our letter immediately. The key is that inquiries should be written not only concisely and clearly to the point, but also courteous and helpful.

　　An inquiry can usually be divided into three parts. In the first part, tell our supplier how we obtain his/her name and why we write the letter to him/her. In the second part, introduce our own business, including the goods we need, the quantity we want, the terms of trade we prefer and so on. In the third part, state the response we hope for a prompt reply to receive. End our letter with a complementary close.

　　The reply to an inquiry should be prompt and courteous and cover all the information that asked for. Otherwise, the inquirer may turn to other suppliers and we may lose a potential customer and business opportunity. In writing a reply to an inquiry, we should express our thanks to the inquirer for his/her interest in our products, then answer the questions asked and provide other relevant and necessary information. Every question should be answered helpfully. In case there is a question we can not answer immediately, or the goods inquired are out of stock, we should inform the inquirer the soonest time we can offer the relevant information, or we can supply the goods. Besides, if the inquiries are the first inquiries, we should also state briefly to them the strengths and advantages of our products.

3.3　Letters for Example

3.3.1　A First Inquiry and Reply

1. A First Inquiry

Vancouver Textiles Corporation
356 Madison Street
Vancouver, Canada

15 November, 2018

China National Textiles Imp. & Exp. Corp.

Shanghai Home Textiles Branch

18 Chung Shan Road

Shanghai, China

Dear Sirs,

We have been informed by the Bank of Canada, Vancouver, that you are one of the leading exporters of textiles in Shanghai and that you wish to extend export business to our market.

You will be pleased to note that we are importers of bed-sheets and other home textile products, having over 20 years' experience in this particular line of business.

At present, we are keenly interested in bed-sheets and shall be glad if you will kindly send us your latest price list for bed-sheets in various colors specifying sizes and designs. If possible, please also rush us samples by airmail for our reference.

In the meantime, we think it necessary to stress the importance of the material of bed-sheets used. Here in Vancouver only all-cotton bed-sheets are salable and any synthetic fiber or blended fiber is not in demand. If the quality of your products comes up to expectations and your prices are attractive, we expect to place regular orders for fairly large numbers. And if you are in a position to meet our demand, we think your products will enjoy popular sales in our market.

For your information, we would like to state that we usually pay for our imports by L/C at sight, which we feel sure will be agreeable to you.

Your early reply will be appreciated.

Yours faithfully,

Tom

VANCOUVER TEXTILES CORPORATION

2. A Reply to the Above Letter

China National Textiles Imp. & Exp. Corporation

Shanghai Home Textiles Branch

Shanghai, China

17 November, 2018

Vancouver Textiles Corp.

356 Madison Street

Vancouver, Canada

Dear Sirs,

Thank you for your letter of 15 November inquiring for bed-sheets, we wish to inform you that the sample-cutting book, price list and catalogue asked for in your above letter have been airmailed you separately. We are confident that these will give you all the details you required. All the items are of good quality and can be supplied in a wide range of designs and colors to meet the requirements in your market. However, if you are in need of any other information not contained therein, please feel free to let us know. We shall satisfy you to the best of our ability.

Your payment terms by L/C at sight are acceptable to us. In order to ensure punctual shipment of the goods to be ordered, please ensure that the covering L/C reaches us at least 30 days before the stipulated time of shipment.

By the way, we wish to inform you that our all-cotton bed-sheets have become very popular on the world market because of their durability and reasonable prices and it has been difficult for us to meet the increasing demand. However, if you place your orders before the 10 December, we assure you of our prompt shipment. We hope that our price will be workable and that business will result to our mutual advantage.

We look forward to receiving your orders soon.

Yours faithfully,

China National Textiles Imp. & Exp. Corp.

Shanghai Home Textiles Branch

Tony Li

3.3.2 General Inquiry and Reply

1. A General Inquiry

Vancouver Textiles Corporation
356 Madison Street
Vancouver, Canada

15 November, 2018

China National Textiles Imp. & Exp. Corp.
Shanghai Home Textiles Branch
18 Chung Shan Road（E.1）
Shanghai, China

Gentlemen,

We have read your advertisement in *China Daily* and are glad to know you are an important exporter of textiles in your country.

We shall appreciate it if you can send us a copy of your catalogue, with details of your prices and terms of payment. We should find it most helpful if you could also provide some samples of the various types.

In view of the demand for your products, an immediate reply is appreciated.

Truly yours,

Tom

---

2. A Reply to the Above Letter

China National Textiles Imp. & Exp. Corporation
Shanghai Home Textiles Branch
Shanghai, China

---

17 November, 2018

Vancouver Textiles Corp.
356 Madison Street
Vancouver, Canada

Gentlemen,

We are very pleased to receive your inquiry of 15 November and enclose our illustrated catalogue and price list giving the details you asked for. Also by separate post, we are sending you a full range of samples and when you have an opportunity to examine them, you will agree that the goods are both excellent in quality and reasonable in price.

On regular purchases in quantities of not less than five hundred of individual items we would allow you a discount of 10% and a special discount of 5% of net price for payment within 10 days after receipt of invoice. If you place your order not later than the end of this month, we would guarantee delivery within 14 days after receipt.

We look forward to receiving your first order.

Truly yours,

Tony Li

3.3.3 Specific Inquiry and Reply

1. Inquiry

Vancouver Textiles Corporation
356 Madison Street
Vancouver, Canada

15 November, 2018

China National Textiles Imp. & Exp. Corp.

Shanghai Home Textiles Branch

18 Chung Shan Road

Shanghai, China

Gentlemen,

Re: "White Healthier" cloth

We are now considering buying large quantities of your "White Healthier" cloth which could be made into ladies' skirts. There is always a ready market here for cloth, provided it is of good quality and competitive in price. We should be thankful if you would send us its full details concerning the prices, discounts, terms of payment, delivery date, and packing and so on. It would also be appreciated if you send us your samples.

We used to purchase this article from other sources, but we now prefer to buy from your company, because we are given to understand you are able to supply larger quantities at more attractive prices. Besides, we have confidence in the quality of Chinese products. If your terms are favorable, we shall probably order about 10,000 meters. If your "White Healthier" cloth agrees with the taste of our market, we feel confident of placing a trial order with you.

We look forward to hearing from you by return.

Yours faithfully,

Tom

2. Reply

China National Textiles Imp. & Exp. Corporation

Shanghai Home Textiles Branch

Shanghai, China

17 November, 2018

Vancouver Textiles Corp.

356 Madison Street

Vancouver, Canada

Gentlemen,

Re: "White Healthier" cloth

We acknowledge with thanks receipt of your letter of 15 November, inquiring about our "White Healthier" cloth.

We have pleasure in sending you a copy of the catalogue and samples of the full range of colors and the prices. They will reach you within next week. You will see detailed information about "White Healthier" cloth on page 3 of the catalogue.

Besides, the "White Healthier" cloth is packed in plastic bags, with 1 piece in each bag, 10 bags to a paper box, 20 boxes to a carton reinforced by hook iron. We give 10% discount on orders of $25,000 or more and payment should be made by Confirmed Letter of Credit payable by draft at sight. Our time of delivery is within 30 days after receipt of your L/C.

We should be very pleased to do business with you and would ask you to let us have the usual trade and bank references. We hope the catalogue gives all the information you need. If you find the above acceptable, please cable us for confirmation. And if you need any further details, please do not hesitate to write us again.

Yours sincerely,

Tony Li

3.4 Words and Phrases

1. **inquiry** *n.* (or enquiry) act of requesting information on the availability of specific product 询盘；询价；查询

2. **quotation** *n.* statement of the price of a certain product 报价单

3. **request** *n.* act of asking for sth. in speech or writing, esp. politely （口头或书面的）要求；（尤指）请求

4. **commodity** *n.* article, product or material that is exchanged in (esp. international) trade

商品；货物；（尤指国际贸易中的）物品、产品或材料

    5. **correspondence**　*n.*　letter-writing, letters　通信；信件

    6. **sample**　*n.*　a part that is representative of a whole　样品

    7. **acknowledge**　*v.*　accept the truth of (sth.), admit (sth.)　承认（某事物）属实；供认（某事物）

    8. **lasting**　*adj.*　to continue to exist for a long time or forever　持久的；耐久的

    9. **critical**　*adj.*　crucial　关键的

    10. **out of stock**　脱销

    11. **textile**　*n.*　(esp. pl) woven or machine-knitted fabric　织物；纺织品

    12. **for one's reference**　供某人参考

    13. **in the meantime**　同时

    14. **stress**　*v.*　put stress or emphasis on (sth.)　着重；强调（某事物）

    15. **synthetic fiber**　人造纤维；合成纤维

      blended fiber　混合纤维

    16. **comes up to**　达到；符合

    17. **therein**　*adv.*　in that place　在那里；在其中

    18. **punctual**　*adj.*　happening or doing sth. at the agreed or proper time　按时的；准时的；守时的

    19. **stipulate**　*v.*　state (sth.) clearly and firmly as a requirement　讲明；规定（某要求）

    20. **craftsmanship**　*n.*　skilled workmanship　技艺；手艺

    21. **appeal to**　有吸引力；有感染力

    22. **irrevocable**　*adj.*　that cannot be changed or revoked, final　不可撤销的

    23. **payable**　*adj.*　that must or may be paid　可支付的；应支付的

3.5　Notes

1. **inquire**　*v.*　咨询；询问；询价，常与 about 和 for 连用。

e.g.　Many foreign customers are inquiring about our products.
　　　很多外商询问我们的产品。

　　　Thank you for your fax of July 24 inquiring for our Model YN-116 machine tool.
　　　感谢你方 7 月 24 日询问我方 YN-116 型机械工具的传真。

    2. **We have been informed by the Bank of Canada, Vancouver, that you are one of the leading exporters of textiles in Shanghai.**　加拿大银行温哥华分行告知我们，贵公司是上海的主要纺织品出口商之一。

    3. **having over 20 years of experience in this particular line of business**　对该业务有 20 年的经验

    4. **your latest price list for bed-sheets in various colors**　你们各种颜色的床单的最新价

格单

5. rush=send immediately 立即递送

rush us samples by airmail 赶快航寄样品

e.g. Please rush us your latest catalogue.

请赶快将你方最新目录寄给我们。

6. We think it necessary to stress the importance of the material of bed-sheets used. 我们认为必须强调一下床单所用料子的重要性。

7. order *n.* 订单

v. 订购；订货

e.g. Place a large order with you.

向你方大量订货。

If you allow us 10% discount, we will order 10,000 dozen.

如果你方给予 10%的折扣，我们将订购 10 000 打。

名词 order 常与动词 make、send、place 等连用，如果表示订购某项货物，后接"for"，也可接"on"或"of"，但"for"最为常见。

e.g. If your price is in line, we will send you an order for 500 sets.

如果你方价格与市价相符，我们将订购 500 台。

8. If you are in a position to meet our demand, we think your products will enjoy popular sales in our market. 假如贵方能够满足我方的要求，我们认为你方产品能在我方市场畅销。

9. We would like to state that we usually pay for our imports by sight L/C, which we feel sure will be agreeable to you. 我们要告知贵方，我们对进口货一般用即期信用证付款并认为贵方会认同这一点。

10. catalogue 商品目录

一般由卖方将其要出售的商品编印成目录，并标注商品价格和有关运输的信息。通常情况下，目录表上的价格无法律效力。

11. be of good quality=the quality is good 质量上乘

12. If you are in need of any other information not contained therein, please feel free to let us know. 假如你们需要这里没有包含的任何信息，请随时让我们知晓。

feel free to do sth. 随意做某事；欢迎你……

类似的表达方式有：Please do not hesitate to do sth. 请毫不犹豫地做某事。

e.g. If you have further questions, please feel free to ask us.

如果你们有任何其他的问题，请随时向我们询问。

Please do not hesitate to contact us if you need help.

如需要帮助，请立即与我们联系。

13. reasonable 合理的

类似的表达方法有：

realistic 符合实际的；现实的

workable 可行的

in the line with the present market　与现行价格相符

e.g.　Our price is quite reasonable.
　　　我方价格是相当合理的。

14. **meet one's demand**　满足某人的需求

15. **Our all-cotton bed-sheets have become very popular on the world market because of their durability and reasonable prices and it has been difficult for us to meet the increasing demand.**　我们的全棉床单因其经久耐用和合理的价格已十分畅销，我们难以满足日益增长的需求。

16. **mutual advantage**　双方的利益

17. **We should find it most helpful if you could also supply some samples of the various types.**　如果贵方能提供各种产品的样品就最好不过了。

18. **CIF**　价格术语 "Cost，Insurance and Freight"，成本、保险加运费的缩写，通常称作 "到岸价"。

19. **discount**　*n.*　折扣；折价；贴现。

折扣是指在交易的过程中卖方给予买方的价格减让，一般按原价的百分比来计算。国际贸易中使用的折扣名目较多，除一般折扣外，还有为扩大销售而使用的数量折扣（quantity discount），为某种特殊目的而给予的特殊折扣（special discount）以及年终回扣（turnover bonus）、付现折扣（cash discount）等。折扣与佣金一样，有 "明扣" 和 "暗扣" 之分。明扣通常是在价格条款中明确表示出来的，如："US\$ 280.00 per M/T CIF Bombay less 3% Discount."。

allow (or: give, make, grant) ××% discount off (on) the prices of goods　按货价给予 ××% 的折扣

e.g.　If you order 5,000 sets, we would grant you 10% discount.
　　　如果你方能订购 5000 台，我们将给予 10% 的折扣。
　　　We give 10% discount for cash payment.
　　　现金付款，我们予以九折优待。

at a discount　低于正常价格；打折扣

e.g.　The goods are selling at a discount.
　　　该货正以低价销售。

20. **terms of payment**　支付条件，也可以说 payment terms，指经买卖双方协商后，在交易合同中对付款条件做出的明确具体的规定。付款条件主要包括使用的货币、付款金额、支付方式等内容。

21. **delivery date**　交货期

其他表达方式有：date of delivery, time of delivery, delivery time, date of shipment, time of shipment, shipment time (date), etc.

22. **profitable**　*adj.*　有益的；有利的；可获利的

profitable fields of investment　有利的投资场所

profit　*n.*　（常用复数）利润

net profits　净利润；纯利润

total profits 总利润

profit ratio (rate) 利润率

gross profits 总利润；毛利

sell sth. at a profit 出售某物而获利

23. **appeal to the most selective buyer** 吸引最挑剔的买主

24. **Letter of Credit payable by sight draft** 即期信用证，也可以说 L/C available by sight draft.

Letter of Credit 信用证，为可数的普通名词，在商业书信中常用大写，单数为(a) Letter of Credit，复数为 Letters of Credit，且常用大写缩写形式，即(a) L/C 和 Ls/C。当用 credit 表示信用证时，复数为 credits。

by sight draft 凭即期汇票支付

a draft at sight=a sight draft

25. **a ready market** 销路好；畅销，也可用 there is a good market for 或 popular、well-sold。

26. **provided they are of good quality and competitive in price** 只要物美价廉

　　provided=on condition that 只要

e.g.　I'll agree to go provided that my expenses are paid.
　　　只要我的费用被付清，我就同意离开。

27. **from other sources** 从其他渠道（从其他供货商）

28. **agree with=suit** 适合；符合

e.g.　If your shirts agree with the taste of our market.
　　　如果你们的衬衫符合本市场的口味的话。

　　　The humid climate didn't agree with him.
　　　他不适应潮湿的气候。

　　　The color doesn't agree with my taste.
　　　这种颜色不符合我的口味。

29. **feel confident=be sure of** 有信心

　　place a trial order=place an order for trial 试订

e.g.　We feel confident of placing a trial order with you.
　　　我们有信心向你们订购一批试销。

We feel confident of doing sth. 我们有信心做某事。

类似的表达方法有：

We are confident that…

We have confidence in …

30. **by return** 书信中常用语，也可以说 by return mail，表示收信后立即回信。

31. **We acknowledge with thanks receipt of your letter.** 收到来信，表示感谢。属于比较正式的行文，相当于 Thank you for your letter。

32. **full range of colors and prices** 全套颜色和价格

range 范围，系列

e.g.　Our leather products of "Rose" range are selling fast in Canada.

我们的"玫瑰"系列皮革产品在加拿大很畅销。

33. trade and bank references　商业和银行证明人

在首次与买主做交易时，卖方往往需对买方进行资信调查，以确定交易风险的大小，并决定采用何种付款方式。了解对方资信的渠道通常有两个，一个是买方的开户银行，另一个是与买方有业务往来的公司。

3.6　Useful Expressions

1. 询盘

(1) Please quote us for the goods listed on the enclosed inquiry sheet, giving your prices CIF Shanghai. Please also state your earliest delivery date, your terms of payment and discounts for regular purchases.

请向我们报出列在被附询盘表中货物的上海到岸价格，并且请说明你方对于常规购买的最早交货期、支付条件和折扣。

(2) We have pleasure in enclosing our inquiry for handmade gloves in leathers, against which you are requested to make us an offer on CIF basis.

我方很高兴地附上我们皮革手工手套的询盘，这是应你方请求做出的以到岸价为基础的发盘。

(3) We shall be pleased if you will furnish us with your lowest quotation for the following goods.

如果贵方为我方提供下列产品的最低报价，我们将会很高兴。

(4) Please let us know on what terms you can supply the above goods.

请告知我方贵方以什么交易条件供应上述商品。

(5) We are pleased to inform you that there is good sale for your Drilling Machine, Model Z-33 and would ask you to send us your best offer. If your price is found competitive, we are confident there are good prospects for business.

我们很高兴地告知你方，贵方型号为 Z-33 的钻机很畅销，并请求你方报此钻机的最优惠价格。如果你方所报价格具有竞争力，相信我们能够达成交易。

(6) As we are in the market for canned mushroom, we should be pleased if you would send us your best quotations.

我公司拟购罐装蘑菇，如果你方能够向我们发送你方最优报价，我们将非常高兴。

(7) If you think this offer is acceptable to you, please fax us immediately for our confirmation.

如果你方认为此报价是可以接受的，请立即向我方发出传真以便我们确认。

2. 索取

(1) Will you please send us a copy of your catalogue, with details of your prices and terms of

payment?

你方能向我方发送一份带有贵方详细价格和支付条件的目录吗？

(2) Will you please send us a copy of your catalogue and current price list for bicycles? We are interested in bicycles for both men and women, and also for children.

你方能向我方发送一份贵方自行车的目录和最新价格表吗？我们对男式、女式以及儿童的自行车感兴趣。

(3) Please send us your catalogue and the information about your plastic toys advertised in *the Time* Magazine of 11 November, 2012.

请向我们发送你们于 2012 年 11 月 11 日在《时间》杂志上刊登广告的塑料玩具的目录和相关信息。

(4) We have seen your advertisement in the *Foreign Trade* and should be glad if you would send us by return patterns and prices of good quality cottons available from stock.

我们已经看到了贵方在《对外贸易》上的广告，如果你方能够向我们寄送现有存货中优等棉花的来样和价格，我们将非常高兴。

(5) We expect to receive a copy of your latest catalogue giving the details of your export prices and terms of payment, together with samples.

我方希望获得贵公司的最新产品目录和有关出口价格、付款条件以及样品的详细资料。

(6) Kindly let us have the description of your electric hedge trimmers.

请贵公司寄来电动修剪机的说明书。

3. 答复

(1) We thank you for your inquiry of 13 November and are pleased to send you our quotation for leather shoes and handbags.

我们感谢你方 11 月 13 日发来的询盘且很高兴地向你方发送我们的皮鞋和皮包的报价。

(2) We were pleased to know from your letter of 24 October of your interest in our products and enclose the catalogue and price list giving the details you asked for. Also enclosed you will find details of our conditions of sale and terms of payment.

我们很高兴地从你方 10 月 24 日的来信中获悉你方对我们的产品感兴趣，随附的目录和价格单给出了你方所需的详细资料。我们的销售和支付条件的详细资料也已附函寄出。

(3) Thank you for your inquiry and for your interest in our products.

感谢贵方询价以及对我方产品感兴趣。

(4) In response to your letter of 15 July inquiring for bed-sheets, we wish to inform you that the sample-cutting book, price list and catalogue asked for in your above letter have been airmailed you separately.

作为对你方 7 月 15 日对床单询盘来信的回复，我们想通知你们贵方在上封信要求的剪样本、价格单和目录已经被分别航邮给你们了。

(5) We invite your attention to our other products, details of which you will find in the catalogue, and look forward to receiving your first order.

我们提请贵方关注我方的其他商品，它们的详细信息可以在商品目录上找到，期待贵方的首次订购。

(6) Thank you for your letter of October 15, 2012. As requested, we are submitting our quotation in triplicate and hope you to place an order with us as early as possible.

感谢你方 2012 年 10 月 15 日的来信。应你方要求，我们呈上三份我们的报价，希望贵方尽快和我们确定订单。

(7) We are making you the following offer, subject to your reply reaching here within 5 days.

在你方回复到达我方五天之内，我们做出如下报价。

3.7　Exercises

1. Choose the best answer.

(1) We feel sure that they will be glad to furnish you _____ any information you require.

  A. for   B. at   C. on   D. with

(2) We look forward to _____ your catalogue and price list for women's sweater.

  A. receive B. receiving C. received D. being received

(3) Quotations and samples will be sent _____ receipt of your specific inquiries.

  A. for   B. upon   C. with   D. to

(4) As this article falls _____ the scope of our business activities, we take this opportunity to express our wish to conduct some transactions with you in the near future.

  A. with   B. in   C. within   D. at

(5) We assure you _____ our full cooperation.

  A. for   B. at   C. with   D. of

(6) We thank you for your letter dated May 6 _____ our silk blouses of various styles.

  A. inquiry for B. inquiring for C. inquired for D. inquire for

(7) They are seriously considering _____ a complete plant for the production of cutting tools.

  A. import B. importing C. to import D. imported

(8) Will you please send us your prices for the items _____ below.

  A. listing B. being listed C. to list D. listed

(9) If you can supply us the goods immediately, we shall _____ to place a prompt trial order.

  A. preparing B. be preparing C. prepare D. be prepared

(10) These leather handbags are fully illustrated in the catalogue and are _____ the same high quality as our gloves.

  A. for   B. of   C. to   D. in

2. Fill in the blanks.

Dear Sirs,

Re: Sample Cost

We really appreciate your ___(1)___ cooperation during the past several years. We think we have developed a beneficial trade ___(2)___ your area ___(3)___ the basis of equality and mutual benefit. We hope that we will reach a bigger turnover ___(4)___ the coming years.

As ___(5)___ the new samples of our products, our statistics showed that we had a very heavy burden ___(6)___ sample cost. As you know, during the past years we always supplied small quantity ___(7)___ samples to our customers free ___(8)___ charge. We not only had to pay the samples' cost, but also pay for the postage ___(9)___ express couriers, such as UPS, FedEx. However, our profit is getting smaller and smaller owing ___(10)___ the uprising prices of raw materials. ___(11)___ such circumstance, we find it is getting difficult to run business in this way. In order to solve this problem ___(12)___ a reasonable way, we hope our customer could help to share the cost ___(13)___ paying the postage. So could you please inform us your account number of UPS or FedEx or other express ___(14)___ return? So that we could send samples by your account number, while we will supply the samples free of charge in normal small quantity ___(15)___ before.

We hope that our request will gain your approval.

Yours sincerely,

3. Translate the following sentences into English.

（1）请报给我们你方 FOB 上海最具竞争力的价格，并将报价单发送至……

（2）我们对你方报价单里的彩笔感兴趣，请寄报价单来。

（3）我们随函附上每件货物的照片和规格，相信贵方能按照我方要求生产并报出最优惠的价格。

（4）求购种花工具，请寄带价目表的商品目录以供我们参考。

（5）如果这一切都可能，能否请你们在 2 月 1 日之前给我们一个回复？

（6）为了给你们提供更多有关我公司的信息，我们随函附上我们最新的宣传册供你方参考。

（7）能否告知我方，超过 100t 后的订单的折扣是多少？

（8）请对上述产品报运至我方工厂交货的最低价格。

（9）请详细告知贵公司经营的主要商品情况及成交条件。

（10）如果你方报价可以接受并且非常令人满意，我们会向你们定期下订单。

（11）我们是世界上最大的丝绸进口商之一。我们过去一直是从日本进口，现在转向中国市场订购。

（12）因事务紧急，我方盼望能在本周内收到贵公司的复函。

4. Translate the following sentences into Chinese.

(1) As requested, we now offer you 500 tons of walnut meat as follows.

(2) If you think this offer acceptable, please cable us immediately for our confirmation.

(3) The offer remains firm to the end of this month.

(4) If your order is large enough, we can allow you a higher discount on our price.

(5) We now offer you, as requested, as follows, which is subject to our final confirmation.

(6) We are enclosing herewith an inquiry sheet.

(7) As soon as we have received your inquiry, we will immediately mail you the samples and offer you most favorable prices.

(8) Please quote as requested in our inquiry sheet your lowest prices and state the earliest delivery date.

(9) We are making you the following offer, subject to your reply reaching here within five days.

(10) Though the quality of your textile is satisfactory for us, your quotation is not quite in line with the present market.

(11) Your lowest quotations are requested, by return, for the under-mentioned goods.

(12) If you are in a position to supply the goods as per the attached inquiry at very competitive prices, we trust large orders will be obtained.

5. Translate the following letters into English.

1）关于人工制皮包的询盘

> 敬启者：
>
> 　　从意大利贸易指南中看到你公司的广告，获悉你公司正在生产并出口各类人工制真皮皮包。我公司是中国最大的百货公司之一，深信价格公道的优质皮包在本地区是有稳定需求的。
>
> 　　请贵公司尽快惠寄各类产品的详细资料，包括尺码、颜色与最新价目单，并请附寄用各种材料制成的样品，以及最优惠的价格为盼。
>
> 　　我公司渴望了解贵公司的资信情况，盼早日回复。
>
> 敬上

2）关于人工制皮包询盘的复信

> 敬启者：
>
> 　　你公司询价人工制皮包的来函收悉，谨表谢意。
>
> 　　今随函寄上我公司人工制皮包的最新价格表和有图片的商品目录，以便贵公司了解

我司详情。此外，另函邮寄样品一批，从中你会发现：我公司以最低的价格向你方提供优质商品，相信定会获得你公司的惠顾。

　　我公司还生产各类人工制皮手套，质量与皮包一样好，在商品目录中有详尽说明，望你公司也感兴趣。如需要，请来函，定照你公司要求寄上相关材料。

Answers for Reference

Chapter 4   Offers

4.1   Introduction

An offer is a promise to supply goods on the terms and conditions stated. It is usually made either by way of advertisements, circulars and letters or in reply to inquiries. It must be made and accepted before a contract can exist. Offers, however, should be made with accuracy. In the end of the offer, it always concludes with an expression of hope that the offer will be accepted. In international business, offers can be divided into two kinds: firm offer and non-firm offer.

An offer is called a "firm offer" if it is a definite promise to sell and the terms in the promise will not be changed if it is accepted by a buyer within the given valid time. A firm offer should be expressed clearly, definitely, completely and finally in words, as when it takes the form of a letter; or it may be implied, as when it takes the form of a quotation that contains the words " for acceptance within 7 days ", or similar qualifying words. In making a firm offer, mention should be made of the time of shipment and the mode of payment desired; in addition, an exact description of the goods should be given and, if possible, pattern or sample sent. A firm offer is capable of acceptance and once it has been accepted it cannot be withdrawn. It is the buyer's option to accept or reject or counter-offer during the validity period. No reputable seller would risk his reputation by withdrawing his offer before the stated or agreed time.

Non-firm offers are the ones which are not binding upon the sellers and the details of the offers may change in certain situations. It always contains the words like "subject to seller's confirmation" "subject to our approval" "to offer without engagement (obligation)" etc.

4.2   Writing Guide

An offer should include the following parts:
(1) an expression thanking for the inquiry, if any;
(2) name of commodities, quality, quantity, and specification;
(3) details of prices, terms of payment, commissions, or discounts, if any;
(4) packing and date of delivery;

(5) the validity of the offer;

(6) favorable comments on the goods themselves;

(7) an expression of hopes for an order.

4.3　Letters for Example

4.3.1　Letter One

China National Import & Export Corp.

Hebei Road
Tianjin, China

November 1, 2018

Greenwood Textiles Co., Ltd.
315 Lens Road
London, England

Dear Sirs,

　　We thank you for your inquiry of October 15. As requested, we are airmailing you, under separate cover, one catalogue and sample books for our Tianjin printed pure silk fabrics. We hope they will reach you in due course and will help you in making your selection. In order to start a concrete transaction between us, we take pleasure in making you a special offer as follows:

　　Article: No.8002 Tianjin Printed Pure Silk Fabrics
　　Design: No.46839-2A
　　Specification: 30×36
　　Minimum: 20,000 yards
　　Packing: In bales or in wooden cases, at seller's option
　　Price: US $54 per yard CIF London
　　Shipment: To be made in three equal monthly installments, beginning from January 2019.
　　Payment: By confirmed L/C payable by draft at sight to be opened 30 days before the time of shipment.

　　We trust the above offer will be acceptable to you and await with keen interest your trial order.

Yours faithfully,
China National Import & Export Corp.
Manager

4.3.2 Letter Two

China National Import & Export Corp.

Hebei Road

Tianjin, China

November 1, 2018

Greenwood Textiles Co., Ltd.

315 Lens Road

London, England

Dear Sirs,

Thank you for your letter of September 30. As you know, the quality of our products is excellent, and during the past few years we have supplied our goods to dealers in several tropical countries. In compliance with your request, we are making you the following offer:

Art No. T1258	USD68.50 Per Set CIF3 Dubai
Art No. T1356	USD15.60 Per Set CIF3 Dubai
Art No. T1436	USD30.20 Per Set CIF3 Dubai
Art No. T1789	USD25.50 Per Piece CIF3 Dubai

Minimum Order Quantity: one 20' FCL container for each Art No.

Packing: Art No. T1258, 1 set per carton, total 150 cartons to a 20'FCL.

Art No. T1356, 12 sets per carton, total 150 cartons to a 20'FCL.

Art No. T1436, 8 pieces per carton, total 150 cartons to a 20'FCL.

Art No. T1789, 10 sets per carton, total 150 cartons to a 20'FCL.

Shipment: To be made within one month upon receipt of relevant L/C.

Payment: By confirmed L/C payable by draft at sight.

Insurance: To be covered by the seller for 110% of the invoice value against All Risks and War Risk.

As the prevailing price in the international market is fluctuating drastically, our offer remains valid for only one week. If you accept it, please let us have your reply as soon as possible.

We look forward to your favorable reply.

Yours faithfully,

China National Import & Export Corp.

Manager

4.3.3   Letter Three

China National Import & Export Corp.

Hebei Road

Tianjin, China

November 1, 2018

Greenwood Textiles Co., Ltd.

315 Lens Road

London, England

Dear Sirs,

Thank you for your inquiry of October 10. We also confirm having received your sample.

We have carefully examined the sample and can assure you that we are able to produce articles of identical type and quality. Based on your annual requirement, we are making you the following offer:

Men's Box			
Calf Shoes (brown)	Sept.	100 pairs	$15.00pr.
---ditto---(black)	Immediate	100 pairs	$15.50pr.
Ladies' kid			
Tie Shoes	Sept.	100 pairs	$14.50pr.
Ladies, Calf			
Court Shoes	Oct.	100 pairs	$14.00pr.

Net price, FOB London

All items for which we have quoted are made from very best quality leather and can be supplied in a range of designs and colors wide enough to meet the requirements of a fashionable trade such as yours.

We look forward to receiving your order.

Yours sincerely,

China National Import & Export Corp.

Manager

4.3.4　Letter Four

China National Import & Export Corp.

Hebei Road
Tianjin, China

November 1, 2018

Greenwood Textiles Co., Ltd.
315 Lens Road
London, England

Dear Sirs,

Thank you for your inquiry of September 30 for our Trial Grabber brand bicycles. In reply, we take pleasure in offering you as follows:

Item#			Unit Price
032340	20"	men's	US$ 55.00
032341	20"	women's	US$ 57.00
042340	26"	men's	US$ 56.00
042341	26"	women's	US$ 58.00

Payment:　　By Letter of Credit in seller's favor.

Delivery Date:　　Within 60 days after receipt of your order.

The above prices are on a CIF London basis. Please note that commissions are not allowed but a 5% discount applies to orders for each item exceeding 2,000.

We manufacture and export 8 models of bicycles which are well-known for their solid frame, reasonable price and attractive design. If you are interested in other models, please see the enclosed illustrated catalogue.

We look forward to your order.

Sincerely yours,
China National Import & Export Corp.
Manager

4.3.5　Non-firm Offer

China National Import & Export Corp.

Hebei Road
Tianjin, China
November 1, 2018

Greenwood Textiles Co., Ltd.
315 Lens Road
London, England

Dear Sirs,

Your letter of October 10 asking us to offer you the cotton shirts has received our immediate attention. We are pleased to be told that there is a great demand for our products in London.

In compliance with your request, we are making you the following offer subject to our final confirmation.

Commodity: Cotton shirts different colors and pattern assortments
Size: Large(L), Medium(M), Small(S)
Packing: Shirts are wrapped in plastic bags and packed in standard export cardboard cartons
Price: CIF London per dozen in RMB, L: 45, M: 42, S: 35
Payment: By confirmed L/C payable by draft at sight.

We hope the above will be acceptable to you and await with interest your early order.

Yours faithfully,
China National Import & Export Corp.
Manager

4.4　Words and Phrases

1. **offer**　*n.*　an act of proposing to sell certain goods or services at specific prices on certain terms and conditions　报盘；出价

2. **firm offer**　实盘

3. **non-firm offer**　虚盘

4. **sales by description**　凭说明书买卖

5. **destination**　*n.*　the place to which one is going or directed　目的地

6. **valid**　*adj.*　legally acceptable　有效的

e.g.　The quotation remains valid for three days.
该报价有效期三天。

7. **bid** *n.* 递价；出价；递盘（由买方发出）

　　　　　 v. 递盘

8. **take advantage of** 利用

9. **after receipt of = after we receive…= upon (on) receipt of：** 收到……之后

e.g. Upon (on) receipt of your L/C, we will send the goods.

10. **subject to** 以……为条件；以……为准

11. **make allowance** 折让

4.5　Notes

1. **acknowledge** *vt.* 告知收到，常用于国际商务信函的起始句

e.g. We acknowledge receipt of your letter of June 15.
　　　6 月 15 日的来信已收到。

　　　Please acknowledge this cheque as soon as you receive it.
　　　收到该支票后，请立即告知。

2. **Printed Pure Silk Fabrics** 印花纯丝细布

3. **subject to your reply reaching here before June 12** 以贵方的答复于 6 月 12 日之前到达我方为准

这是实盘中常用的语句，说明报盘的有效期。Subject to：以……为条件（为准），在报盘信中常用该句式来表明该盘的性质。

e.g. Subject to our acceptance
　　　以我方接受为准（表示此报盘为虚盘）

　　　Subject to your acceptance within two weeks
　　　以贵方在两周之内接受为条件（说明此报盘为实盘）

4. **Please note that…** 请注意……

这是商业信函中常用的句型，用以提醒收信人对信中的某一内容予以特别关注。

e.g. Please note that the market for the goods is rising and our price cannot remain
　　　unchanged for long.
　　　请注意，目前这种产品的市场行情看涨，我们的价格不会保持很长时间。

5. **5% discount applies to orders for each item exceeding 2,000.** 对每一种型号的产品订货超过 2000 台可得 5%的折扣。apply to 意为"适用于"。

6. **by confirmed L/C payable by draft at sight** 凭保兑的、即期汇票付款的信用证

7. **take pleasure in doing…** 高兴地做……

较正式的客套语，也可以用以下句型：

take (have) the pleasure of doing…

take (have) the pleasure to do…

8. **as requested** 根据要求

9. **item No.**　商品编号

10. **description**　货名

11. **drum**　*n.*　铁罐

12. **offer subject to sample approval**　报盘以样品确认为准

13. **subject to our final confirmation**　以我方最后确认为准

4.6　Useful Expressions

1. Referring to your inquiry of November 20, we have quoted as below.

依据贵方 11 月 20 日的询盘，兹报价如下。

2. We were very pleased to receive your inquiry of 3 March and now confirm our cable of this morning, as follows:

很高兴收到贵方 3 月 3 日的询盘，今晨确认回电如下：

We have pleasure in offering (quoting) you the following goods:

我们很高兴向贵方对如下产品报价。

3. In order to meet your demand, we should recommend an excellent replacement. It is as good as the required article in quality but the price is 20% lower. It has found a ready market in Southeast Asia.

为满足贵方要求，现推荐一种优良的代用品。在质量上它和您所询购的商品一样好，但价格要低 20%，该产品在东南亚已很畅销。

4. Our prices are highly competitive when you consider the quality.

如果贵方考虑质量的话，我们的价格是很有竞争性的。

5. We take pleasure to enclose our offer No. UE-1109 for your consideration. The price we quoted is on FOB Tianjin basis instead of on either FAS Tianjin or CIF Hongkong basis and that our offer will be valid until August 31, 2018.

我方很高兴向贵方就编号为 UE-1109 的产品做出发盘。我们所报价格是 FOB 天津的价格，而不是 FAS 天津或是 CIF 香港的价格，我们的报价在 2018 年 8 月 31 日之前有效。

6. In view of our long-standing business relationship, we would like to allow you another 2% commission for further promotion of our products.

考虑到我们之间长期的贸易关系，我方愿再给贵方 2%的佣金以进一步推销我们的产品。

7. All quotations are subject to our final confirmation unless otherwise stated.

所报价格，除特别注明外，须经我方确认后方能生效。

8. We quote for this article US $10 per case FOB Shanghai.

我方报此货 FOB 上海价，每箱十元。

9. It's better for us to have a talk on price terms, because it is one of the key points in our dealings.

我们最好先讨论价格条款，因为它是我们交易中的关键因素。

10. As the prices quoted are exceptionally low and likely to rise, we should advise you to accept the offer without delay.

由于所报价格特别低并可能涨价，我方建议贵方立即接受此报盘。

11. We desire to call your attention to our special offer. You will readily understand that this offer is good only for acceptance reaching us before the end of January. In view of the heavy demand for this line, we advise you to send orders as soon as possible.

希望贵方能对该特殊的报盘引起注意。贵方将会明白在一月末之前接受这一报盘是非常有利的。由于该产品的需求量很大，我方建议贵方尽快订货。

12. Thank you for your kind cooperation in meeting our demands. We hope you will furnish us with further mutually profitable offers in the future.

感谢贵方合作，满足了我们的要求。希望贵公司将来能进一步向我方报出互惠的价格。

13. We trust you will find our offer satisfactory and look forward to receiving your order.

我方相信贵公司会对我方的报盘感到满意，期望收到贵方的订单。

4.7 Exercises

1. Choose the best answer.

(1) If you are interested, we will send you a sample lot, _____ charge.

    A. within   B. for   C. in   D. free of

(2) We are making you our quotation for shoes _____.

    A. as follows   B. as following   C. as follow   D. following

(3) We have been _____ with that firm for many years.

    A. making business   B. contacting   C. dealing   D. supplying

(4) We are prepared to keep the offer open _____ 25 this month.

    A. in   B. on   C. to   D. until

(5) We will withdraw the offer if we should not hear _____ you by the end of this week.

    A. of   B. from   C. by   D. to

(6) As our products are of high quality and at moderate price, they _____ fast sales in the international market.

    A. have   B. get   C. enjoy   D. make

(7) Your prompt rely _____.

    A. will be highly appreciated   B. will be thanked

    C. is to be thanked   D. is appreciated high

(8) We assure you that you will find a ready sale _____ this type of new product.

    A. to   B. for   C. on   D. in

2. Translate the following sentences into English.

（1）同时，我方很高兴向贵方报喷墨打印机最有竞争力的价格如下。

（2）由于价格合理，质地优良，我们的棉布销售很快。

（3）兹函复，报不锈钢餐具的价格如下。

（4）我方做出如下报盘，以3日内收到贵方回复有效。

（5）贵方3月18日询价函已收到，谢谢，现报盘如下。

（6）如对我方报价感兴趣，请告知。

3.Translate the letter given below into Chinese.

Dear Sirs,

We are glad to make you a competitive offer as follows:

      Name of commodity: Seagull Brand Camera

      Quantity: 2,000 sets

      Price: at USD200 per set CIFC3% New York

      Packing: packed in cartons

      Time of shipment: for shipment during March/April 2018

      Terms of payment: by confirmed L/C payable by sight draft

The above offer is firm subject to your reply reaching us before the end of this month.

Your prompt reply is highly appreciated.

Yours faithfully,

Answers for Reference

Chapter 5   Counter offers

5.1   Introduction

If a buyer does not agree with any or some of the transaction terms of a quotation or a firm offer, he sent a counter offer. A counter offer is virtually a partial rejection of the original offer and also a counter proposal initiated by the buyer or the offerer. The buyer may show disagreement to the price, or the packing, or shipment and state his own terms instead.

When the receiver disagrees with the offer sent to him or her and makes some changers, the changed one is called a "counter offer", while the original one, when expired, will be replaced by the counter offer. In the counter offer, the buyer may show his disagreement to the certain term or terms and state his own idea instead. Such alterations, no matter how slight they may appear to be, signify that business has to be negotiated on the renewed basis. The original offer or the seller now becomes the offeree, and he has the full right of acceptance or refusal. In the latter case, he may make another counter offer of his own. This process can go on for many rounds till business is finalized or called off.

If it is amended again, another counter offer is made until an acceptable one is worked out. This final and accepted offer is firm and legally binding to both parties. It is not uncommon for a business negotiation to go through several rounds of offers and counter offers before an agreement is reached.

In making a counter offer, one has to state the terms most explicitly and use words very carefully so as to avoid ambiguity or misunderstanding, the same way as one usually does in making an offer.

When a buyer rejects an offer, he should write and thank the seller for his trouble and explain the reason for rejection. Not to do so would show a lack of courtesy.

5.2   Writing Guide

If the offer is rejected or partially rejected, a letter of rejection or a counter offer is to be written, which should include:

(1) an expression of thanks for the offer;

(2) express regret at inability to accept;

(3) reasons for inability to accept the offer;

(4) your own terms and conditions upon which business is likely to materialize;

(5) a wish of business opportunities in future.

5.3 Letters for Example

5.3.1 Letter One

A. B. Greenwood & CO., LTD.

315 Lens Road
London, England

June 4, 2018

China National Import & Export Corp.
Tianjin, China

Dear Sirs,

We thank you for your offer of 1 June for 25,000 yards of rayon/woolen mixed fabric and 23,000 yards of dyed cotton shirting.

We immediately contacted our customers and they showed a great interest because there is a growing demand for cotton textiles. The prices you quoted, however, are found too much on the high side. ABC company, one of our customers, told us that they would possibly take up your entire stock of dyed cotton shirting, provided that the material was offered lower than 95p a yard. ABC is one of the leading garment manufacturers in our country, so there is a good chance of finalizing an order with them if the present price can be lowered to meet their requirement. We hope you will take advantage of this chance so that you will benefit from the expanding market.

As for the rayon/woolen mixed fabric, our customers hold a fairly large stock at present because of large shipments recently received from Hong Kong. You will, however, receive orders from us soon because we are sure the recent brisk demand will deplete our stock before long.

In these circumstances, we are most anxious that you will do your utmost to reduce the price for dyed cotton shirting and we await your reply with great interest.

Yours faithfully,
A .B . Greenwood & CO., LTD.
Manager

5.3.2 Letter Two

A. B. Greenwood & CO., LTD

315 Lens Road
London, England

February 24, 2018

China National Import & Export Corp.
Tianjin, China

Dear Sirs,

We wish to thank you for your letter of the 20 Febuary, offering us 50 long tons of the captioned goods at USD 105.00 per long ton CIF London, usual terms.

In reply, we very much regret to state that our end-users here find your price too high and out of line with the prevailing market level. Information indicates that the sugar of England market have been sold at the level of USD 98.00 per long ton.

Such being the case, it is impossible for us to persuade our end-users to accept your price, as good of similar quality is easily obtainable at a much lower figure. Should you be prepared to reduce your limit by, say 8%, we might come to terms.

It is in view of our long-standing business relationship that we make you such a counter offer. As the market is declining, we hope you will consider our counter offer most favorably and fax us acceptance at your earliest convenience.

We are anticipating your early reply.

Yours faithfully,
A .B . Greenwood & CO., LTD.
Manager

5.3.3　Letter Three

China National Import & Export Corp.

Hebei Road
Tianjin, China

March 15, 2018

Greenwood Textiles Co., Ltd.
315 Lens Road
London, England

Dear Sirs,

　　Thank you for your letter of March 11. We are disappointed to hear that our price for the captioned goods is too high for you to work on.

　　Much as we would like to cooperate with you in expanding sales, we are regretful that we just can't see our way to entertain your counter offer, as the price we quote is rather realistic. As a matter of fact, we have received a lot of orders from various sources at our level.

　　If you could accept our price after careful consideration, please do let us know. On account of a limited supply available at present, we would ask you to act quickly.

　　We are looking forward to your early reply.

Yours sincerely,
China National Import & Export Corp.
Manager

5.3.4　Letter Four

China National Import & Export Corp.

Hebei Road
Tianjin, China

April 5, 2018

Greenwood Textiles Co., Ltd.
315 Lens Road
London, England

Dear Sirs,

We acknowledge receipt of your letter dated April 2. In the letter you asked us for more favorable terms. We regret that at the present moment, we are unable to offer more than the terms agreed upon last year. Apart from the fact that our margin of profit would be quite narrow, there is the additional problem of maintaining our retail prices at a competitive level.

We, nevertheless, are willing to give you a discount on larger orders and enclose a list of the lines with the appropriate discount against each one.

We hope that these generous discounts will bring about a substantial order.

We look forward to hearing from you soon.

Yours sincerely,
China National Import & Export Corp.
Manager

5.3.5　Letter Five

A. B. Greenwood & CO., LTD.

315 Lens Road
London, England

June 29, 2018

China National Import & Export Corp.
Tianjin, China

Dear Sirs,

We have received your offer of June 26 and regret that you have turned down our counteroffer.

As we are in urgent need of the goods and anxious to conclude the business with you, we have made our every effort to persuade our client to accept your offer of \$35.00 per piece. Fortunately, our customer in Vancouver has changed his mind and approached us again with an order for 3,000 dozens of the above goods on your terms.

We are very pleased to have been able to finalize this initial business with you after protracted exchange of correspondence, and look forward to your sales contract, upon receipt of which, we will open the relative L/C without delay.

Yours faithfully,

A .B . Greenwood & CO., LTD.

Manager

5.4 Words and Phrases

1. **counter offer**　还盘

2. **amend**　*v.*　to alter formally by adding, deleting, or rephrasing　修正；修改

3. **quote**　*v.*　to tell a customer the price you will charge them for a service or product　报价；报盘

e.g.　to quote sb. a price for sth.

4. **provided(that)**　*conj.*　on condition of ; if　如果；假设

e.g.　We accept your offer provided (that) shipment is made in the first half of the year.

5. **garment**　*n.*　a piece of clothing　服装

6. **indicate**　*v.*　to show that a particular situation exists or that something is likely to be true　指出；表明

7. **parcel**　*n.*　quantity dealt with in one transaction; a lot　批

8. **in view of**　鉴于；考虑到……

9. **see one's way to do sth.**　有可能或有意办某事

10. **supply**　*v.*　give or provide something needed or asked for　供货；提供

　　　　　n.　the amount, especially of a commodity, provided or available　供给

e.g.　Supply goes over demand.

11. **enclose**　*v.*　to put something inside an envelope as well as a letter　封入；随封

5.5　Notes

1. **rayon/woolen mixed fabric**　人造丝羊毛混纺织品

   dyed cotton shirting　染色棉细布

2. **The prices you quoted, however, are found too much on the high side.**　你方报价太高。

   On the high side = rather high　偏高

3. **There is a growing demand for cotton textiles.**　对棉织品的需求日益增长。

   growing = increasing　增加的

4. **They would possibly take up your entire stock of dyed cotton shirting, provided that the material is offered lower than 95p a yard.** 如贵方染色棉细布报价能低于 95 便士/码，他们可买下贵方的全部存货。

   take up = accept　接受

5. **There is a good chance of finalizing an order with them.**　有与他们达成交易的好机会。

   finalize = complete　完成；达成；确定

   e.g.　finalize one's plans

6. **...the recent brisk demand will deplete our stock before long.**　最近需求活跃，存货不久将告罄。

   brisk demand　需求活跃

7. **We are most anxious that you will do your utmost to reduce the price.**　我们希望贵方尽最大可能降低价格。

   do your utmost　尽最大可能

8. **the captioned goods**　标题所列货物

   类似表达还有：the subject article(goods), the goods(article) mentioned in the subject line

9. **out of line with the prevailing market level**　与目前市场水平不一致

   out of line with the market　与市场水平不一致

   in the line with the market　与市场水平一致

10. **keen competition**　激烈的竞争

11. **say 8%**　比如说 8%，say 此处指"比方说，就是说"

12. **entertain your counter offer**　考虑接受贵方还盘

13. **On account of a limited supply available at present, we would ask you to act quickly.** 由于目前只有少量现货可供，希望贵方尽快做出决定。

14. **margin of profit**　获利空间

    e.g.　If you could lower the price by 5%, then it would allow a good margin of profit.
    如果贵方能将价格下降 5%，那么就会获利丰厚。

15. **turn down**　回绝；拒绝

    e.g.　They turned down his proposal.

16. **conclude the business**   达成交易

e.g.   We are glad to have concluded this transaction with you.
　　　 我们很高兴和你们达成了这笔交易。

也可用 close business、finalize the business、come to terms、close a deal、come to business、close a bargain 来表示达成交易。

5.6   Useful Expressions

1. Our counter offer as follows:
我方还盘如下：

2. The profit margin for these products is so thin that any price reduction would make business transactions pointless.
这些产品的利润很薄，任何降价都会使生意失去意义。

3. We have cut our price to the limit. We, regret, therefore, being unable to comply with your request for further reduction.
我们已经将价格降至极限，因此，很遗憾无法同意贵方要求再次降价的请求。

4. We are sure no other buyers have bid higher than this price.
我们确信没有别的买主的出价高于此价。

5. We are not in a position to entertain business at your price, since it appears to be on the high sight.
由于价格过高，我们恐怕无法按此价格成交。

6. We have accepted your firm offer. I'm afraid the offer is unacceptable.
我们已经收到了贵方报的实盘。我方恐怕无法接受贵方的报价。

7. We would be willing to discuss a volume discount if your order volume is doubled.
如果贵方的订货量能翻一番，我们将乐于与贵方讨论批量订货的折扣问题。

8. We regret to inform you that we cannot accept your offer, as we are obtaining the same quality from other sources at a price 6% lower than yours.
很遗憾，我们不能接受贵方的报盘，因为我们从别的渠道获得的同等质量产品的报价比贵方的低 6%。

9. Your offer is unacceptable unless the price is reduced by 5%.
除非你方降价 5%，否则我们无法接受报盘。

10. Much as we would like to avail ourselves of the offer made to us, we find it impossible to accept owing to your price being about 10% higher than the average.
尽管我们非常想接受贵方给我们的报价，但由于贵方的价格高于平均价格 10%让我们无法接受。

11. Considering the quality of the suitcases offered, we do not feel that the prices we quoted are at all excessive, but in view of the long-standing business relations between us, we have decided

to offer you a special discount of 2% for an order exceeding $ 20,000.

考虑到我们所提供的箱子的质量，我们认为所报价格一点都不高，但是鉴于我们之间的长期业务关系，我们决定对贵方超过 2 万美元的订货给予 2%的特别折扣。

12. Since our prices are closely calculated, we regret being unable to grant the discount you asked for.

因为我们的价格经过精密的计算，所以我们很遗憾不能给予贵方所要求的折扣。

13. We can offer you a substitute which is at the same price and of similar quality to the goods ordered.

我们可以为贵方提供的产品与贵方所订购的产品价格相同、质量相近。

14. The goods you ordered are now out of stock. We suggest you substitute No. 26, which is excellent value for the price. Shall we ship the substitute, or would you prefer to wait until we obtain the goods?

贵方所订购的货物现已售完，建议贵方用 26 号货物代替，该货物价格极为划算。我方是否可以装运替换品，还是贵方愿意等待所订货物到位？

15. Your price is quite in line, but the time of shipment is too distant.

贵方的价格很合理，但装运期太远。

16. Owing to heavy commitments, we regret that we cannot entertain any fresh orders for the captioned goods.

由于订货太多，抱歉我方无法接受标题项下货物的任何新订单。

17. We will keep your inquiry before us and as soon as we are in a position to accept new orders, we will contact you by cable.

我们将记住贵方的询价，一旦能接受新订单，一定与贵方电报联系。

18. As this is the case, there is no alternative for us but to cancel the order, which you will please note.

鉴于此，本公司不得不取消订单，敬请知晓。

19. We are always at your service.

我方随时为贵方服务。

5.7　Exercises

1. Fill in the blanks with suitable prep.

We regret to inform you ____(1)____ our quotation has increased ____(2)____ 20% due ____(3)____ the advance of price ____(4)____ the raw materials and the production cost. In order to execute your order smoothly, we calculated the total volume and weight ____(5)____ your orders. We confirm that we can use 1*40"HQ to ship all the goods ____(6)____ your two orders. Please note ____(7)____ we must arrange shipment ____(8)____ the end of this year, because the export drawback rate will be reduced by 4% ____(9)____ Jan. 1, 2018, which means next year's quotation will still rise. If you can accept our properly adjusted price, we'll use 1*40" HQ ____(10)____ ship these two orders ____(11)____ December. If you separate these two orders to use 2*20" containers, then one order will exceed the largest VOLUME ____(12)____ 1*20" container. So we are waiting ____(13)____ your final confirmation. Thank you ____(14)____ advance ____(15)____ your cooperation!

2. Translate the following sentences into Chinese.

(1) The highest discount we can allow on this article is 10%.

(2) As per your request, we have marked the cases with gross, tare and net weights.

(3) We regret to say that we can't accept your offer, as your price is found on the high side.

(4) We hope you will see your way to accept September shipment.

(5) If you cannot accept our offer, please make the best possible counter offer.

3. Translate the following sentences into English.

（1）我们已把价格降到底线，因此很遗憾不能按照贵方要求再降价。

（2）贵方还盘与现行市场价格不符。

（3）由于库存短缺，抱歉我方不能接受贵方的续订单。

（4）原材料价格上涨，我方无法接受贵方降价 10%的还盘。

（5）希望贵方将来能向我方提供更优惠的报价。

4. Write a letter according to the following notes.

贵方向客户所作报价，客户回信中认为价格偏高。给客户回信，信中应包含以下几点内容：

（1）确认收到买方的还盘函并表示遗憾；

（2）提出还盘：可以接受对方降价 9%的要求，但必须确保订购额在 5000 美元以上，因为生产成本明显增加，但质量标准不变；

（3）敦促对方接受。

Answers for Reference

Chapter 6   Conclusion of Business

6.1   Introduction

One of the difficulties in business transaction is to ensure that the two sides have identical understanding of what is being communicated. It is particular important at the time when the bargain is being made that two sides should make sure to have identical understanding of terms to which they are agreeing. And that is why letters confirming the conclusion of transaction are necessary. When writing such letters, make sure of each point being correct and fully understood even if this means going over the whole ground time.

When buyers agree with the term of an offer, they usually place an order — a formal request to sellers for the purchase of certain goods, at a specified quantity. An order can be an acceptance of an offer or sent voluntarily by a buyer. It should be clearly and accurately written out and state all the terms of transaction. According to commercial law, an order is not binding on either party until it is accepted. Then a Sales Confirmation may be worked out by both parties on the basis of terms and conditions provided in the order. In sending out Sales Contract or Sales Confirmation, special attention should be paid to the price, terms of payment, specifications, quality, quantity, time of delivery, port of destination, etc.

There are times when sellers can't accept buyers' orders because the goods required are not available or prices and specifications have been changed. In such circumstances, letters rejecting orders must be written with the utmost care and with an eye to goodwill and future business. It is advisable to recommend suitable substitutes, make counter offers and persuade buyers to accept them. On receiving an order, if the seller agrees with the terms and is in a position to supply the required goods, he will give the buyer an acceptance, a formal statement indicating his assent. Thus the deal is concluded.

6.2   Writing Guide

6.2.1   Order

An order mainly involves:
(1) full details of description, quantities;

(2) price (unit price and total value), terms of payment;

(3) mode of package;

(4) port of destination and time of shipment.

6.2.2   Acceptance Letter

A letter of acceptance often includes:

(1) expression of receiving the order;

(2) favorable comments on the goods ordered;

(3) assurance of prompt delivery and careful attention;

(4) introduction of other products which may be interested by the buyer;

(5) hope for further orders.

6.3   Letters for Example

6.3.1   Letter One

A. B. Greenwood & CO., LTD.

315 Lens Road
London, England

Nov. 18, 2018

China National Import & Export Corp.

Tianjin, China

Dear Sirs,

    Thank you very much for your offer dated Nov. 9. Having discussed with our chairman of the board, we decide to accept your terms and conditions and place a trial order for the four items mentioned in our attached Order Form. We will place regular orders with you as long as the quality is up to our expectation.

    This order is subject to non-delay shipment before Chinese New Year — Spring Festival.

    Enclosed please find our Order Form.

We look forward to your early reply.

Yours faithfully,

A.B. Greenwood & CO., LTD.

General Manger

Encl.

A. B. Greenwood & CO., LTD.

315 Lens Road

London, England

Order No. 345

ORDER FORM

14 November, 2018

Tianjin Imp. & Exp. Corp.

TIANJIN, China

Qty	Item			Catalogue No.	CIF Sydney NET
248	Bed Sheets,	120cm,	red	65	$ 3.5 each
248	Bed Sheets,	105cm,	yellow	98	$ 4.6 each
356	Pillow Cases,		blue	205	$ 2.6 a pair
356	Pillow Cases,		primrose	210	$ 2.6 a pair

Packing: In cotton cloth bales.

Shipment: Prompt shipment from Tianjin.

Payment: By L/C available by a draft at sight.

for W. SANYANG & CO., LTD.

Secretary

6.3.2　Letter Two

China National Import & Export Corp.

Hebei Road

Tianjin, China

March 12, 2018

Greenwood Textiles Co., Ltd.

315 Lens Road

London, England

Dear Sirs,

We are very pleased to receive your order No.345 for Bed Sheets and Pillow Cases. We confirm supply of the goods at the prices stated in your order No.345. It is our honor to have the opportunity of serving you and we are sure that you will be satisfied with the quality of our goods.

Our sales confirmation No. ABC418 in two originals were airmailed to you. Please sign and return one copy of them for our file.

It is understood that a letter of credit in our favor covering the goods should be opened immediately. We wish to point out that stipulations in the relative L/C must strictly conform to the terms stated in our Sales Confirmation so as to avoid subsequent amendments. You may rest assured that we will effect shipment without delay on receipt of your letter of credit.

We appreciate your cooperation and look forward to receiving your further orders.

Yours faithfully,

China National Import & Export Corp.

Manager

6.3.3   Letter Three

Greenwood Textiles CO., LTD

315 Lens Road

London, England

Sep. 27, 2018

China National Import & Export Corp.

Tianjin, China

Dear Sirs,

We thank you very much for your quotation of 24 Sep. and the sample sweaters. We find both qualities and prices satisfactory and are pleased to place an order with you for the following:

15 doz. knitted sweater, small, US$50.00 per doz.
30 doz. knitted sweater, medium, US$60.00 per doz.
20 doz. knitted sweater, large, US$70.00 per doz.
Packing: each sweater to be packed in a polybag, per dozen in a tin-lined carton, with 10 dozens to a wooden case.

Other terms as per your quotation.

We expect to find a good market for these sweaters and hope to place further and larger orders with you in the near future.

Our usual terms of payment are cash against documents and we hope they will be acceptable to you. Meanwhile should you wish to make inquiries concerning our financial standing, you may refer to our bank.

The Standard Chartered Bank, London.

Please send us your confirmation of sales in duplicate.

Yours faithfully,
Greenwood Textiles Co., Ltd.
Manager

6.3.4　Letter Four

China National Import & Export Corp.

Hebei Road
Tianjin, China

June 8, 2018

Greenwood Textiles Co., Ltd.
315 Lens Road
London, England

Dear Sirs,

We are very pleased to receive your order and confirm that all the items required are in stock. It is a pleasure to have the opportunity of supplying you and we are sure that you will be satisfied with the quality of our goods.

Your method of payment, a draft at sight under L/C is quite acceptable to us. On receiving your credit from the bank we will make up your order and will make shipping advice as soon as the shipment is completed. We assure you that this order and further orders shall have our immediate attention.

Yours faithfully,

China National Import & Export Corp.

Manager

6.4 Words and Phrases

1. **order** *n.* an instruction to a tradesman or manufacturer to supply goods; the goods (to be) supplied 订单

2. **sales confirmation** 售货确认书

3. **stipulation** *n.* something specified as the terms of an agreement, contract, etc. 规定

4. **polybag** *n.* 塑料袋；胶带

5. **tin-lined carton** 衬锡纸箱

6. **as per** 按照

7. **stock** *n.* 存货

e.g. This store keeps a large stock of toys.
这家商店备有大量玩具。

8. **place/cancel/reinstate/confirm an order** 开/取消/恢复/确认订单

9. **original** *n.* 正本
    adj. 正本的

10. **airmail** *n.* 航空邮件
    v. 用航空邮件寄送

11. **conform** *v.* 使一致；符合

6.5　Notes

1. **Order Form**　订单

　　regular order　经常性订单

2. **This order is subject to non-delay shipment before Chinese New Year — Spring Festival.**　该订单中所订货物必须在中国的春节前毫无延误地启运。

3. enclosed　随信附着……

4. **in duplicate**　一式两份

　　in triplicate　一式三份

　　in quadruplicate　一式四份

一式四份及其以上也常说 in four copies、in five copies… 或 in four folds, in five folds …

5. **state**　*v.*　陈述；说明

e.g.　Please quote us your lowest price FOB New York, stating the earliest shipment and the packing.

　　　请报最低 FOB 纽约价，并说明最早装运期和包装情况。

6. **for one's file**　以便某方存档，也可以用 for one's record (s)

7. **relative**　*adj.*　有关的；相关的

the relative L/C　相关的信用证，也可以用 the relevant L/C 或 the covering L/C

8. **avoid subsequent amendments**　避免以后的修改

9. **a trial order**　试购单；试订货

6.6　Useful Expressions

1. Thank you for your quotation of June 24 and the sample scarves you sent us. We are pleased to place our order with you as follows:

感谢你方 6 月 24 号的报价和寄来的围巾样品。我们很高兴向你方订货如下：

2. We have the pleasure of placing an order with you for 1,500 dozen blouses at US$ 260 per dozen CIF New York, based on your catalogue No. 66 of December 25.

我们很高兴按你方 12 月 25 日目录本向你方订购 1500 打女士衬衣，每打 260 美元，CIF 纽约价。

3. We thank you for sending your catalogue and price list. We enclose the Order Form and would be grateful if you would send the goods as soon as possible.

感谢你方寄来目录本和价目表。现随函寄去我们的订单，如你方能尽早发来货物，我们将不胜感激。

4. We enclose a trial order. If the quality is up to our expectation, we shall send further orders in the near future.

我方随附试购单，如贵方产品质量达到我方期望，我方未来将有大量订单。

5. Please follow our shipping instructions carefully and make sure that our order is executed to the satisfaction of our customers with the least possible delay.

请认真遵守我们的装船指示，确保毫不延误地执行我方订单以令客户满意。

6. If this first order is satisfactorily executed, we shall place further orders with you.

如果首订单圆满完成，我方将会有续订单。

7. We thank you for your quotation and have noted the price and terms are acceptable, and we accordingly request you to put all items in hand as soon as possible.

感谢贵方的报价，我们认为价格及有关条款可接受，因此请贵方尽快备好所有货物。

8. Your order is booked and will be handled with great care. Please open the relevant L/C, which must reach here one month before the date of shipment.

贵方订单已经确认且将被认真履行。请开立相关信用证且必须在装船前一个月到达我方。

9. Your order is already being carried out/executed/processed, and delivery will be made in accordance with your instructions.

我方正在处理你方订单，并将按照你方要求发货。

10. Your order is receiving our immediate attention, and you can depend on us to effect delivery well within your time limit.

我方非常重视贵方订单，我方将在限期内尽快发货。

11. Delivery will be made immediately on receipt of your letter of credit.

一旦收到你方信用证将立即发货。

12. With reference to your letter of 4 December, we have pleasure in informing you that we have booked your order for 2,000 alarm clocks. We are sending you our S/C No.100 in duplicate, one copy of which please sign and return for our file.

据贵方 12 月 4 日来信，我方很高兴地通知贵方 2000 台闹钟订单已确认。现寄去我方第 100 号销货确认书一式两份，一份签字后请寄回以便我方存档。

13. We highly appreciate your letter of June 24 together with your Order No.567. We are pleased to accept your terms and conditions. Enclosed please find our Sales Confirmation No.56 in duplicate, one copy of which please sign and return to us for our file.

十分感谢你方 6 月 24 日的来信及你方第 567 号订单，我们很乐意接受你们的条款和条件。现随函寄去第 56 号售货确认书一式两份，请签字并回邮一份供我方备案。

14. We trust that this initial order will lead to further dealings between our two companies.

我们相信这第一笔订单会使我们两家公司之间的生意源源不断。

15. While thanking you for your order, we have to explain that without supplies we have no alternative but to decline your order.

非常感谢贵方的订单，需要说明的是，因无货源，我方不得不取消你方订单。

6.7 Exercises

1. Choose the best answer.

(1) We regret to say that the prices you have bid are too low to_____.

    A. not accept   B. be acceptable

    C. be accepting   D. be unacceptable

(2) We can not _____ our offer open for more than three days, so would you please email your acceptance.

    A. have   B. place   C. remain   D. leave

(3) We shall be glad if you will _____ the matter at once and let us know the reason for the delay.

    A. look on   B. look for   C. look after   D. look into

(4) _____ your prices are right, you will find a ready market for the products.

    A. Should   B. To provide   C . Provided   D. Provide

(5) We hope that you will entrust us with more orders when you are again _____.

    A. in the market   B. on the market

    C. out of the market   D. at the market

(6) Please ship the ten chests of tea _____ our Order No.201221 at an early date.

    A. covered by   B. covering   C. to be covered   D. which covered

(7) We assure you that any further orders you may _____ will always be carefully attended to.

    A. place us   B. place with us   C. make us   D. make with us

(8) Your prompt attention _____ our order will be much appreciated.

    A. of   B. for   C. to   D. in

(9) We trust that you will _____ our order with special care.

    A. refer to   B. deal in   C. dispose of   D. attend to

(10) We suggest that shipment of our order _____ effected in May instead of June.

    A. is   B. will be   C. is to be   D. be

2. Translate the following sentences into Chinese.

(1) We'd like to cancel the order for your cultured pearls of the change in the domestic market.

(2) All these items are urgently required by our client. Therefore, we hope that you will make delivery at an early date so that they can sell them out before Christmas.

(3) We shall arrange for dispatch by the first available liner upon receipt of your sight L/C.

(4) With reference to your order of July 6 for musical instruments, we wish to inform you that the goods are in production and will be ready for shipment by the end of October.

(5) We hope that you will be satisfied with this shipment and we look forward to your regular

order in the near future.

3. Translate the following sentences into English.

（1）虽然现时市价较前有所提高，考虑到咱们的长期合作关系，本公司仍会按以往订单所列条件接受此次订单。

（2）现给贵方寄去我方第 123 号销售合同一式两份以供贵方签署。请签署后退回一份留作我方存档之用。

（3）很抱歉，此货物现在已无存货，大概 12 月左右开始有新货供应。当有新货可供时，我们将尽快通知你。

（4）若你方能保证在 11 月 20 日前将货物从青岛运到新加坡，我方乐意向你方订购下列货物。

（5）我们对你方产品的质量和价格均感到满意，现寄去试订单，请供应现货。

4. Translate the letter given below into English.

敬启者：

样品已于 3 月 21 日收到，谢谢。我们对你方的半导体很感兴趣，如果你们能接受 SM-377 型每台上海船上交货价 15 美元，请寄形式发票来。我们准备在本周订货 100 台。收到形式发票后，我们马上开立信用证。

请保证所交货物质量与样品相同。

如果这批试订单货物令人满意，随后将有大批订货。

望早日回复。

此致敬礼

Answers for Reference

Chapter 7 Terms of Payment

7.1 Introduction

With the rapid development of international trade, terms of payment play more and more important roles in international settlement. International business transactions are more complicated than domestic ones. The payment process is much longer, and involves all kinds of risks. Terms of payment define the conditions under which the seller and buyer agree to settle the financial amount of the sales contract. The exporter normally expects to receive payment immediately after delivery of the goods, meanwhile, the importer expects that he will be able to pay off the trade debt only after the goods are sold. So, choosing appropriate terms of payment will be beneficial to exporter and importer.

In international trade, the basic methods of payment can be classified into three categories, i.e., remittance, collection and letter of credit. Remittance and collection are both terms of payment based on commercial credit, while L/C is based on bank credit.

7.1.1 Remittance

Remittance is the simplest method of payment, which refers to that the remitting bank, at the request of a remitter (importer), sends the required funds to a payee (exporter or beneficiary) by means of T/T, M/T or D/D instructed by the remitter, through the paying bank (the overseas branch or the correspondent bank of the remitting bank).

1) Mail Transfer (M/T)

The buyer gives money to a local bank which sends a trust deed for payment to its correspondent bank at the seller's end by mail and entrusts it to pay money to the seller.

2) Telegraphic Transfer (T/T)

It is also named as cable transfer or wire transfer. At the request of the buyer, a local bank sends a trust deed for payment by cable directly to its correspondent bank at the seller's end and entrusts the bank to pay money to the seller.

3) Demand Draft (D/D)

The buyer buys a draft (check) from a local bank and sends it by mail to the seller, the seller or his appointed person can collect money from the relative bank at his end against the draft sent by the buyer.

Therefore, when the importer makes payment, he can adopt three different ways of remittance which are introduced in the order from the fastest to the slowest.

—T/T (Telegraphic Transfer)

—M/T (Mail Transfer)

—D/D (Demand Draft)

In China's foreign trade, when remittance is adopted, most of business is done through T/T. Telegraphic transfer transmitted through tested cable/telex or SWIFT is the most expensive, but its safety and speed could save substantial interest payment if the fund transferred is huge. Mail transfer by the bank's system is a little safer, but its speed is low. Demand draft sent by the customer himself is the least expensive, but is the slowest form of transmission and the customer also bears the risks of theft, destruction or loss in the mail system.

7.1.2 Collection

The application of collection is set out in the Uniform Rules for Collections. According to URC522, collection means the handling by banks, on instructions received, of documents, in order to: ①obtain acceptance and/or payment; ②deliver commercial documents against acceptance or payment;③deliver documents on other terms and conditions. So collection is an arrangement whereby the seller draws a draft on the buyer, and/or shipping documents are forwarded to his bank, authorizing it to collect the money from the buyer through its correspondent bank.

Collection has two kinds mentioned below: clean collection and documentary collection. Clean collection contains financial instruments only, such as bills of exchange, promissory notes, checks, receipts, or other similar types of documents for obtaining cash. Other documents are sent directly by the exporter to the importer.

Collection on commercial documents is accompanied by financial documents or without financial documents. Only when the draft drawn is paid or accepted, the documents will be released to the importer. So according to the ways the documents to be released to the drawee, documentary collection are classified as follows.

1) D/P (Document against Payment)

The collecting bank is allowed to release the documents to the drawee only against full and immediate payment. D/P falls into two categories, i.e., D/P at sight or D/P after XX days sight. The former means upon first presentation, the buyers shall pay against documentary draft drawn by the sellers at sight. The shipping documents are to be delivered against payment only. D/P after XX days sight means, after the first presenting for acceptance, when the accepted draft matures, the seller presents it for payment, then releasing document to buyer.

2) D/A (Document against Acceptance)

The collecting bank is allowed to release the documents to the drawee only against the acceptance of a draft, which means that the exporter provides trade financing to the importer.

Compared with L/C, the major advantage of the above two terms of payment is the low cost.

However, they are both commercial credit, so both the exporter and the importer face risks.

7.1.3 Letter of Credit

A L/C is a written undertaking by the issuing bank (the agent for the importer) to the beneficiary (the exporter), under which the bank undertakes to pay the beneficiary a sum certain in money within a designated time period and against any stipulated terms and documents. In China, letter of credit is the most common method of payment; most of international trades make use of this method.

There are several types of credits, such as Documentary L/C; Confirmed L/C; Sight/Usance L/C; Transferable L/C; Revolving L/C; Back to Back L/C; Anticipatory L/C; Standby L/C and so on.

L/C is based on banking credit, and guarantees payment to the beneficiary, provided that the terms of credit and documents are met. However, the cost of credit is very expensive, especially for the importer, which has to pay deposits to the issuing bank for opening the L/C.

Cable credit refers to letter of credit issued by the issuing bank, transmitted to the advising bank and then to the beneficiary by telegraphic transmission (telex, fax, SWIFT). Usually the issuing bank provides the advising bank with test key, against which the advising bank can ensure the authenticity of letter of credit. Cable credit costs less time and are commonly used nowadays.

As the development of information technology, SWIFT L/C is becoming one of the most commonly used L/C in international trade settlement. The following tables are definitions of SWIFT telex field. MT700 is the format of issue of SWIFT L/C and MT707 is the format of amendment of SWIFT L/C. "M" and "O" respectively represent mandatory field and optional field.

Format of issue of SWIFT L/C: MT700

M/O	Tag	Field Name	Field Explanation
M	27	SEQUENCE OF TOTAL	page number of total pages
M	40A	FORM OF DOCUMENTARY CREDIT	irrevocable or transferable
M	20	DOCUMENTARY CREDIT NUMBER	assigned by the issuing bank
O	23	REFERENCE TO PRE-ADVICE	reference to pre-advice
O	31C	DATE OF ISSUE	the date of issue
M	40E	APPLICABLE RULES	applicable rules
M	31D	DATE AND PLACE OF EXPIRY	date and place of expiry
O	51A	APPLICANT BANK	applicant bank
M	50	APPLICANT	usually the buyer
M	59	BENEFICIARY	usually the seller
M	32B	CURRENCY CODE, AMOUNT	the currency and value of the L/C
O	39A	PERCENTAGE CREDIT AMOUNT TOLERANCE	percentage credit amount tolerance
O	39B	MAXIMUM CREDIT AMOUNT	maximum credit amount
O	39C	ADDITIONAL AMOUNTS COVERED	additional amounts covered
M	41A	AVAILABLE WITH ...BY...	available with ...by...

Continue

M/O	Tag	Field Name	Field Explanation
O	42C	DRAFTS AT …	sight or days after sight for payment
O	42A	DRAWEE	bank the draft is drawn on
O	42M	MIXED PAYMENT DETAILS	mixed payment details
O	42P	DEFERRED PAYMENT DETAILS	deferred payment details
O	43P	PARTIAL SHIPMENTS	allowed or not allowed
O	43T	TRANSHIPMENT	allowed or not allowed
O	44A	LOADING ON BOARD/DISPATCH/TAKING IN CHARGE AT/FROM…	commercial port loading from
O	44E	PORT OF LOADING/ AIRPORT OF DEPARTURE	port of loading/airport of departure
O	44F	PORT OF DISCHARGE/ AIRPORT OF DESTINATION	port of discharge/ airport of destination
O	44B	FOR TRANSPORTATION TO	destination commercial port
O	44C	LATEST DATE OF SHIPMENT	latest date of shipment
O	44D	SHIPMENT PERIOD	shipment period
O	45A	DESCRIPTION GOODS AND/OR SERVICES	goods description
O	46A	DOCUMENTS REQUIRED	documents required
O	47A	ADDITIONAL CONDITIONS	additional requirement
O	71B	CHARGES	bank charges
O	48	PERIOD FOR PRESENTATION	number of days after shipment allowed
M	49	CONFIRMATION INSTRUCTIONS	allowed or not allowed
O	53A	REIMBURSEMENT BANK	reimbursement bank
O	78	INSTRUCTIONS TO THE PAYING/ ACCEPTING/NEGOTIATION BANK	instructions to the paying/accepting/ negotiation bank
O	57A	ADVISE THROUGH BANK	advise through bank
O	72	SENDER TO RECEIVER INFORMATION	sender to receiver information

Format of amendment of SWIFT L/C: MT700

M/O	Tag	Field Name	Field Explanation
M	20	SENDER'S REFERENCE	Sender's reference
M	21	RECEIVER'S REFERENCE	receiver's reference
O	23	ISSUING BANK'S REFERENCE	issuing bank's reference
O	52A	APPLICANT BANK	issuing bank
O	31C	DATE OF ISSUE	date of issue
O	30	DATE OF AMENDMENT	date of amendment
O	26E	NUMBER OF AMENDMENT	number of amendment
M	59	BENEFICIAR	before this amendment
O	31E	NEW DATE OF EXPIRY	new date of expiry
O	32B	INCREASE OF DOCUMENTARY CREDIT AMOUNT	increase of documentary credit amount

Continue

M/O	Tag	Field Name	Field Explanation
O	33B	DECREASE OF DOCUMENTARY CREDIT AMOUNT	decrease of documentary credit amount
O	34B	NEW DOCUMENTARY CREDIT AMOUNT AFIER AMENDMENT	new documentary credit amount after amendment
O	39A	PERCENTAGE CREDIT AMOUNT TOLERANCE	percentage credit amount tolerance
O	39B	MAXIMUM CREDIT AMOUNT	maximum credit amount
O	39C	ADDITIONAL AMOUNTS COVERED	additional amounts covered
O	44A	PLACE OF TAKING IN CHARGE/ DISPATCH FROM/PLACE OF RECEIPT	place of taking in charge/ dispatch from/place of receipt
O	44E	PORT OF LOADING/ AIRPORT OF DEPARTURE	port of loading/ airport of departure
O	44F	PORT OF DISCHARGE/ AIRPORT OF DESTINATION	port of discharge/airport of destination
O	44B	FOR TRANSPORTATION TO...	destination port
O	44C	LATEST DATE OF SHIPMENT	latest date of shipment
O	44D	SHIPMENT PERIOD	shipment period
O	79	NARRATIVE	narrative
O	72	SENDER TO RECEIVER INFORMATION	send and receive information

7.2　Writing Guide

7.2.1　Understand Your Company's Preference

It is important to understand the usual payment terms of the company. Every company has its own practice to do business. Taking the risks into consideration, companies may prefer the L/C, while companies who have long-term relations with others may use documentary collection or T/T.

7.2.2　Express the Terms of Payment Clearly and Accurately

Terms of payment should be expressed in a clear, concise and correct manner in order to avoid misunderstanding and subsequent trouble. We can make use of different methods to settle payment, taking collection as an example, D/P and D/A have different requirements and restrictions.

7.2.3　Use the Proper Words to Change the Payment Terms

If the expected payment terms are turned down, you should give some advice politely and give the reason for the change.

7.3　Letters for Example

7.3.1　Letter One

{Stating the Terms of Payment（L/C）}

UNIVERSAL TRADING CO., LTD.
Rm 1201-1216 Maying Plaza, 131 Donsfans Road, Shanghai, China
Zip: 200120 Tel: 021-58818844 58818766 Fax: 021-58818840
E-mail: young@universal. com. cn

20 Mar., 2018

TIVOLI PRODUCTS PLC.,
Berstofsgade 48, Rotterdam, the Netherlands,

Dear Mr. Trooborg,

Thank you for your letter dated 18 Mar. We are pleased to get your reply.

We request you to open for our account by airmail with the Bank of China, Shanghai Branch, an Irrevocable and Without Recourse Letter of Credit in favor of our company, to the extent of US$30,000 (US Dollars Thirty Thousand only) available by draft in duplicate drawn on you at 30 days after sight for full invoice value against shipment of 20,000 yards Shanghai Printed Pure Silk Fabrics as per our order No.3154 dated 15 Mar.,2018 accompanied by the following documents:

1. Invoice in triplicate.

2. Packing list in triplicate.

3. Full set Clean Bills of Lading made out to order and endorsed in blank notify Buyers marked freight payable at destination.

4. Evidence of shipment of the said merchandise to be effected on or before the end of June 2018 from Shanghai to San Francisco. Partial shipments are not permitted. Transshipments are not allowed.

5. Marine insurance to be effected by Buyers in San Francisco.

We hereby agree duly to accept the above mentioned draft on presentation, and pay the amount thereof at maturity, provided such draft shall be negotiated within three months from this date.

Yours faithfully,
UNIVERSAL TRADING CO., LTD.

Manager

James Li

7.3.2　Letter Two

{Changing the terms of payment（from L/C to D/P at sight）}

TIVOLI PRODUCTS PLC

Berstofsgade 48, Rotterdam, the Netherlands

Tel: 31 74123721 Fax: 31 74123737 E-mail: chila@www.tvl.com.ntl

25 Mar., 2018

UNIVERSAL TRADING CO., LTD.

FAX: 21 58818840

Dear Mr. Li,

Thank you for your email of March 20, 2018.

We appreciate your cooperation in quotation, but we also advise you to make some adjustments of your terms of payment.

On your sight L/C basis, from the moment of credit issuance to the time to collect from our customers, the tie-up of our funds lasts for about three months. It really constrains our marketing capacity. Moreover, you might be aware of the increasing banking fees here, which is now putting an extremely heavy burden on our finance.

Consequently, we ask for your cooperation in dealing with the problem. Specifically, we request that you grant us D/P at sight. If you need the reference, we will be glad to offer you.

Your prompt and positive consideration of this request would help a great deal.

Yours sincerely,

TIVOLI PRODUCTS PLC

Chila Trooborg

Purchasing Manager

7.3.3　Letter Three

(Requiring payment by D/A)

Big Think Co., Ltd.

255 Huaihai Road, Shanghai, China 200233

15 Feb., 2018

Mopper KmDF

Schubert strasse 28, K-1568,

Hamburg, Germany

Dear Mr. Wang,

We have received with many thanks your letter of 12 Feb., which gives us a competitive and reasonable quotation.

We are pleased to accept your quotation and do business with you. However, after long years of satisfactory cooperation, we are surprised that you still demand D/P. So we wish to draw your attention to the method of payment, and we feel that we are entitled to easier and more convenient terms. Most of our suppliers have been drawing on us by their documentary draft at 30 days sight on D/A basis. We should be grateful if you could make out draft for payment 30 days after sight, and the documents will be handed to us on acceptance.

We hope to work with you for a longer time and look forward to hearing from you.

Yours faithfully,

K. Mopper

Managing Director

7.3.4   Letter Four

(Chang in payment terms)

WAIMING International Trade Co., Ltd.

No.145 BinHai Road, Tianjin, China, 300654

Tel:0086-22-65347265, Fax:0086-22-65347266

26 Apr., 2018

Mr. James Johnson

Jones Corporation

1234 7th Avenue,

Tanpza, Florida 33606

Dear Mr. James,

We thank you for your order No. 6235 for delivery in July/August.

We regret, however, that we have to change the mode of payment. As you know, freight and the cost of materials have risen substantially, and considering your large order, we have to raise funds for our trading, so we hope you could make a concession.

Shipment will be made subject to an advanced payment or payment amounting 30% to be remitted in favour of seller by T/T or M/T, and the remaining part on collection basis, documents will be released against payment at sight. We enjoy a good reputation, and upon receipt of the payment in advance, we shall do all in our power to provide quality goods to you.

We hope the above payment term will be acceptable to you and expect to receive your reply in due course.

Best Regards.

Sincerely yours,

WAIMING International Trade Co., Ltd.

Sales Manager

Li Ming

7.4 Words and Phrases

1. **meanwhile** *adv.* at the same time   同时

e.g.   The rest of the world, meanwhile, is slowing.

2. **classify into**   把……分类为

e.g.   The company might classify customers into several categories according to their historical spending patterns, such as platinum, diamond, gold, silver, and so on.

3. **correspondent**   代理行；往来行；通知行

e.g.   This bank is the correspondent of Bank of China in Boston.

4. **substantial** *adj.*   fairly large   大量的

e.g.   won by a substantial margin

You'll receive a substantial amount of money.

5. **transmission**   *n.*   the act of sending a message, money or document   传递；传输

e.g.   Education represents the transmission of ideology.

6. **make use of**   使用；利用

e.g.   We should make use of the chance.

Any citizen can make use of the public library.

7. **Sight/Usance L/C**   即期/远期信用证

e.g.   I'll open a 120-day Usance L/C for the two thirds of your financing.

8. **in favor of**   支持；赞成；以……为受益人；对……有利

e.g.   The evidence is in favor of the defendant.

We were all in favor of his suggestion.

9. **make out** 起草；写出；开出

e.g. Please make out an agreement with them.

Could you make out a receipt for me?

10. **at maturity** 到期日

e.g. payment at maturity 到期付款

With a bond, you always get your interest and principal at maturity, assuming the issuer doesn't go belly up.

11. **adjustment** *n.* the act of making something different 调整

e.g. The company made an adjustment in my salary.

12. **tie-up** *n.* an interruption of normal activity （资金）占用；冻结

e.g. the tie-up of our fund

v. invest so as to make unavailable for other purposes 占用；冻结

e.g. That will tie up funds and increase costs.

13. **marketing capacity** 销售能力；市场营销能力

e.g. constrain our marketing capacity

This suggests a massive potential programme-making, distribution and marketing capacity.

14. **banking fee** 银行费用；佣金

15. **burden** *n.* weight to be borne or conveyed 负担

e.g. Too much praise is a burden.

16. **payment in advance** 预付货款

e.g. We expect payment in advance on first orders.

7.5 Notes

1. **terms of payment** 支付条件；付款方式

类似的表达方式有：payment terms, mode of payment, method of payment

2. **commercial credit&bank credit** 商业信用&银行信用

3. **pay off the trade debt** 清偿债款

pay off 还清（债）；付清工资解雇（某人）；向……行贿；得到好结果；取得成功

e.g. I'll pay off my debt with this cheque.

Persistence will pay off, so don't give up.

Please pay off my salary as the same as others.

4. **tested cable/telex** 加押电报/电传

5. **SWIFT** Society for Worldwide International Financial Transmission

6. **shipping documents are forwarded to his bank** 将运输单据递交给银行

shipping document 运输单据；货运单据

e.g.   L/C No. should appear on all shipping documents.

7. **forward**   *v.*   send or ship onward from an intermediate post or station in transit   转交；传递

e.g.   Please forward my mail to my new address.

8. **financial instruments**   金融工具；金融票据

e.g.   The Company provides information service for obtaining current market prices on traded financial instruments.

9. **draw a draft/bill on sb.**   开立以某人为付款人的汇票

10. **documents to be released to the drawee**   放单给受票人

11. **release**   *v.*   释放；让与；准予发表

e.g.   The latest developments have just been released to the media.

Life is a prison, death a release.

12. **place an initial order**   试订单

initial order/first order   首批订货；第一次订购

e.g.   We hope that this initial order will lead to further business between us.

13. **an Irrevocable and Without Recourse letter of Credit**   无追索权的不可撤销信用证

14. **in duplicate**   一式两份

in triplicate   一式三份

e.g.   Applications must be made out in triplicate.

申请书必须填写一式三份。

15. **Full set clean Bills of Lading made out to order and endorsed in blank notify buyers marked freight payable at destination.**   全套清洁做成凭指示和空白背书的海运提单通知买方，并注明运费到付。

full set   全套

clean B/L   清洁的海运提单

order and endorsed in blank   凭指示和空白背书

freight payable at destination, Freight to Collect   运费到付

16. **marine insurance**   海运保险

e.g.   Marine insurance contracts are indemnity contracts and require the parties to exercise the utmost good faith.

17. **are entitled to**   有权利……

e.g.   All are entitled to an equal start.

We are entitled to cancel the contract which became overdue owing to the buyer's non-performance.

18. **acceptance**   *n.*   承兑

e.g.   As agreed, we are enclosing our draft at 30 days for acceptance by your bankers.

19. **make a concession**   give in/yield a concession   让步

e.g.   We agree to make a concession and grant you a reasonable compensation.

20. **do all in our power**   尽全力

7.6 Useful Expressions

1. I hope you would leave us some leeway in terms of payment.

我希望你可以在付款方式上通融一些。

2. The telegraphic transfer shall reach the Bank of China at least five days before the delivery date of vessel.

电汇应在船期前至少 5 日到达中国银行。

3. Draft must be accompanied by a full set of original clean on board marine Bill of Lading made out to order, endorsed in blank, marked freight prepaid.

汇票必须附有全套正本的清洁已装船海运提单，凭指示、空白背书，并注明"运费已付"。

4. With regard to terms of payment, we regret being unable to accept documents against payment.

关于付款方式，我们很抱歉不能接受付款交单。

5. We have been doing business with you on the basis of cash against documents(CAD) for over a year and would like to change the payment by 30-day bill of exchange, documents against acceptance.

我们以凭单据付现金的方式和贵公司交易已有一年多了，今后希望能变更为承兑交单凭 30 天汇票支付。

6. 30% will be paid for deposit by T/T before production arranged, the balance is to be paid before shipment.

在开始投入生产前通过电汇方式预付货款的 30%，余款在装运前付清。

7. As agreed we have forwarded our bill, No. 2782 for $1,720.00 with the documents to your bank , Industrial & Commercial Bank of China, Caohejing Branch, Shanghai. The Draft has been made out for payment 30 days after sight, and the documents will be handed to you on acceptance.

按照协议，我方已向你方银行，即中国工商银行上海漕河泾支行，提交第 2782 号跟单汇票金额为 1720 美元，支付方式为 30 天的远期汇票承兑交单。

8. We have taken the liberty of drawing on you today against this consignment for $500,000 at sixty days' sight, which please protect on presentation.

兹向贵公司开具见票后 60 日付款、面额 500 000 美元汇票一张，请予以承兑。

9. Shipment will be effected subject to an advanced payment amounting 30% to be remitted in the seller's favour by T/T, and the remaining part on collection basis, documents will be released against payment at sight.

装运货物系以卖方电汇预付金 30%为前提，其余部分采用托收，即期付款交单。

10. My home office has consent to amend the term of payment in accordance with your request.

我们总公司已同意按你方要求修改支付方式。

11. With an eye to our business prospects, we wish you will change your term of payment. 从我们的业务前景考虑，我方希望贵方改变支付方式。

7.7　Exercises

1. Answer the following questions.

(1) What kinds of terms of payment are there in international trade?

(2) What are the difference between T/T, M/T and D/D?

(3) Does D/P after 30 days sight have more risks than D/A? Why?

(4) What is letter of credit and what are the types of it?

(5) What is the advantage and the disadvantage of payment by L/C?

(6) Besides the three traditional terms, what other methods are used in international trade?

2. Discuss on the following topic.

Most exporters are fond of payment by L/C, however, with the development of international trade, some exporters are willing to use the terms of payment by D/P, factoring, export credit insurance and so on. Discuss under what circumstances, a seller could agree to payment by them.

3. Write a letter.

Suppose you work in China National Textiles Import & Export Corp. Hunan Branch (Address: 65 Wuyi East Changsha 41000, P. R. China). Your company will import a great many textiles from Major Partitions Ltd. (Address: Unit 910 Liberte Street, Candiac, Canada). You are responsible for the business, and you should persuade your customer to change the terms of payment from L/C to D/P at sight. Writer a tactful letter explaining that you have to do this against D/P and why you have to do.

4. Translate the following sentences into English.

（1）为了节省开立信用证的高额费用，我方将在所订购的货物已备齐待运，舱位已订好时，电汇全部金额。

（2）我方认真考虑了你方建议用较宽松的付款方式支付你方订购的货物，鉴于我们之间良好的合作关系，我方同意接受 30 天远期付款交单的支付条件。

（3）很遗憾地通知你方，我方的贸易惯例是不接受承兑交单的付款方式。

（4）由于生意相当萧条，故要求贵方改变付款条件。建议凭 30 天的承兑方式付款，若贵方接受这一条件，请予以确认。

（5）你方须在本合同签订后的 7 天内将合同金额 30%的定金电汇给我方，其余金额以托收方式，即期付款交单支付。

5.Translate the following passage into Chinese.

We are pleased to accept your quotation and do business with you. However, after long years of satisfactory cooperation, we are surprised that you still demand D/P. So we wish to draw your attention to the method of payment, and we feel that we are entitled to easier and more convenient terms. Most of our suppliers have been drawing on us by their documentary draft at 30 days sight on D/A basis. We should be grateful if you could make out draft for payment 30 days after sight, and the documents will be handed to us on acceptance.

Answers for Reference

Chapter 8   Establishment of L/C and Amendment

8.1   Introduction

Letter of Credit is the most frequently used mode of payment in international trade. On one hand, the Letter of Credit can assure the seller of payment if he makes the agreed-upon shipment. On the other hand, it also assures the buyer that he is not required to pay until the seller ships the goods. It is thus a catalyst that provides the buyer and the seller with mutual protection in dealing with each other.

The characteristic of the L/C is: the L/C is a separate document from the basic contract, which is the contract between the issuing bank and beneficiary. Issuing bank provides the guarantee of payment with its credit. The L/C mainly deals with the documents instead of goods, services and so on.

As a sales contract is initiated, the buyer and the seller agree to have payment settled by means of L/C. The applicant (importer) will first request the issuing bank to open an L/C, usually an irrevocable documentary L/C, in favor of the beneficiary (exporter). The issuing bank will examine the credit-worthiness of the buyer before it considers issuing the L/C. The L/C issued by the bank is then passed to the advising bank (exporter's bank) that represents the beneficiary in his country. On receiving the L/C, the beneficiary will check the terms and conditions against the sales contract to ensure that everything agrees with the credit requirement. Then he will make shipment and forward all the documents required by the credit to the advising bank or negotiating bank to get payment. The issuing bank will check the documents against the terms and conditions of the L/C, and debit the account of the applicant and present the document to them.

However, sometimes the importer may have certain reasons to fail to open the credit according to the contract on time. Meanwhile, the exporter cannot ship the goods without receiving the L/C. In such a case, the exporter is obliged to urge the importer to establish the L/C in time in order not to delay shipment.

The exporter, on receipt of the Letter of Credit from the advising bank, should first of all go through all the clauses set forth in the L/C to make sure they are in full conformity with the terms stipulated in the sales contract. It is extremely essential to put this step in an important position.

Any discrepancies, even a minor difference, which is not discovered or amended timely and duly, may lead to the exporter's serious difficulty and the exporter may run the risk of his draft being dishonored by the negotiating bank or the issuing bank. As a result, when there are some discrepancies or some soft clauses which the beneficiary can't accept set forth in the L/C, amendment is necessary. There are other reasons for the L/C amendment, such as an unexpected situation with regard to supply, shipping, etc. The exporter should ask the importer to amend the L/C. In order to leave sufficient time to the seller to produce the shipping documents and to the bank to make their negotiation, the date of shipment and the expiry date of the L/C should be at least two weeks apart. Then the importer will request the issuing bank to send notification of amendment to the beneficiary. Both the seller and the buyer can request to amend the L/C. The common reasons for the L/C amendment are as follows:

(1) to extend the validity time of the L/C;

(2) to extend the validity time for shipment;

(3) to amend the amount of money;

(4) to amend the specification and the name of the commodity;

(5) to amend the name of the shipping vessel;

(6) to amend the mode of transport;

(7) to amend the place of loading and unloading;

(8) to amend some clauses in the L/C.

While dealing with these kinds of problems, courtesy is very important. One often sends a fax to amend and extend the Letter of Credit.

When amendment to the credit is needed, we should pay close attention to the following clauses.

(1) the form of documentary credit;

(2) the date and place of expiry, the latest date of shipment and the period for presentation;

(3) the currency code and amount both in numeral and in capital letters;

(4) the name and address of the importer and the exporter;

(5) the specification and quantity of the goods covered by the credit and shipping mark;

(6) the terms of price including trade terms, freight and insurance premium and so on;

(7) documents required (Draft, Commercial Invoice, Bill of Lading, Insurance Policy, etc.);

(8) partial shipment and transshipment;

(9) name of the place or port of shipment and discharge;

(10) instructions to the negotiating bank, the confirming bank, if any;

(11) the type of risk and the amount of insurance coverage, if required;

(12) the L/C is transferable or non-transferable, if necessary;

(13) soft clauses.

When amending L/C, the following points should be kept in mind by parties concerned.

(1) Once the beneficiary applies for L/C amendment, it is the applicant who is entitled to

decide whether to amend an L/C or not.

(2) In order to avoid additional charges and expenses, the beneficiary should put forward all items being amended at one time.

(3) Once the applicant decides to amend an L/C, the amendment should be issued by the original issuing bank and advised by the original advising bank to the beneficiary.

(4) Usually, a credit can not be amended without the agreement of the issuing bank, the confirming bank, if any, and the beneficiary.

(5) An issuing bank is irrevocably bound by an amendment as of the time it issues the amendment.

(6) A confirming bank may extend its confirmation to an amendment and will be irrevocably bound as of the time it advises the amendment. A confirming bank may, however, choose to advise an amendment without extending its confirmation and, if so, it must inform the issuing bank without delay and inform the beneficiary in its advice.

(7) The terms and conditions of the original credit (or a credit incorporating previously accepted amendments) will remain in force for the beneficiary until the beneficiary communicates its acceptance of the amendment to the bank that advised such amendment. The beneficiary should give notification of acceptance or rejection of an amendment. If the beneficiary fails to give such notification, a presentation that complies with the credit and to any not yet accepted amendment will be deemed to be notification of acceptance by the beneficiary of such amendment. As of that moment the credit will be amended.

(8) A bank that advises an amendment should inform the bank from which it received the amendment of any notification of acceptance or rejection.

(9) Partial acceptance of an amendment is not allowed and will be deemed to be notification of rejection of the amendment.

(10) A provision in an amendment to the effect that the amendment shall enter into force unless rejected by the beneficiary within a certain time shall be disregarded.

8.2　Writing Guide

The following points are the requirements of urging establishment of and making amendment to the Letter of Credit.

8.2.1　Courtesy

Letter of Credit is of much benefit to the exporter, so when the exporter urges L/C establishment or requests amendment to L/C, he should be polite, tactful, thoughtful and appreciative, and avoid irritating, offensive or belittling statements.

8.2.2   Consideration

Traders should emphasize the YOU attitude and positive, pleasant facts. In this way, the seller could remind the buyer to open the Letter of Credit in time.

8.2.3   Clarity

Good diction means the exactness or near exactness. The exporter and the importer should explain themselves clearly, avoid ambiguous sentences and wordy jargon and express statements in well-constructed sentences and paragraphs.

8.3   Letters for Example

8.3.1   Letter One

(Notifying the Beneficiary of the L/C issuance)

MASRI BRO.CO., LTD.
65 Kespuy Street, Dubai

26, Jan., 2018
National Silk Corporation
Tianjin, China

Dear Helen,

We acknowledge receipt of your Sales Confirmation No. AD-MASSCA05 with great pleasure. We have countersigned it and returned one for your file as requested.

In the meantime, as your usual terms of payment is sight L/C, we have instructed our bank, THE NATIONAL BANK OF DUBAI LTD, CAIRO BRANCH, to open the relevant L/C of EUR600, 000 in your favor, which will arrive at your end soon.

Please pay your best attention to the quality of the goods, the delivery time as well as other terms specified in this S/C. If your execution of this order turns out to be satisfactory, regular orders will be placed in the near future.

Yours truly,
MASRI BRO.CO., LTD.
Manager
ALEXANDRIA HASSID

8.3.2   Letter Two

(Urging the Importer to Establish an L/C)

National Silk Corporation
Tianjin, China

6 Feb., 2018
Kee & Co., Ltd.
34 Regent Street,
London, UK

Dear Mr. James,

With reference to the 4,000 dozen shirts under our Sales Confirmation No.SX260, we wish to draw your attention to the fact that the date of delivery is approaching but up to the present we have not received the covering L/C, which should have reached us before 5 Feb., 2018. This has caused us much inconvenience, since we have already got the goods ready for shipment according to our Sales Confirmation.

You may recall that the same thing happened to the execution of our last contract. It was only after the market had turned for the better that you opened the covering L/C, quite beyond the time limit. We should have refused then to effect shipment, but we acceded to your request for fulfillment of your order. At the same time we pointed out that you should take effective measures to prevent the similar occurrence.

This article, as you know, has met with great popularity since offered for sale, and new orders have nearly exhausted our stock. But in view of our long-term business relationship, we are still holding the goods for you.

Please do you utmost to expedite its establishment before 8 Feb., 2018 so that we can execute the order within the prescribed time. Otherwise, we shall have no alternative but to cancel the contract and will not enter into any more transactions with you next year. We regret for this decision, but of course we are in no way to blame.

We are looking forward to your Letter of Credit at an early date.

Yours sincerely,
National Silk Corporation
Manager
(Signature)

8.3.3   Letter Three

(Requesting for L/C Amendment by mail)

To: John.man@keeco.com
From: Helenchen@national.silk.com
Date: 8 Feb., 2018
Time: 3:35:26 pm
Subject: Amendment to the L/C No. AN/VS0615ILC

Dear Mr. John,

We have received your L/C No.AN/VS0615ILC issued by the Citibank for the amount of $28,720 covering 2,500 dozen Men's Shirts. After reviewing the L/C, we regret to find that there are certain points that do not comply with the terms of our Sales Confirmation No. HL08GS103.

1. Our S/C No. HL08GS103 emphasizes that your Letter of Credit shall allow transshipment, but the Credit states: "transshipment prohibited".

2. Your credit calls for shipment in two equal monthly lots during May/June, 2018, whereas it is explicitly stipulated in the S/C that shipment is to be made in a single lot not later than May 31, 2018.

3. There is no word "about" before the quantity and amount in the L/C, although the word is clearly used before them in our S/C.

4. Your L/C stipulates the proportion of the goods in an assortment of Types A, B, C is 20%, 40%, 40% respectively. But the assortment contracted for is Types A 30%, B 30%, and C 40%.

You are requested to make the necessary amendments without any delay, as the shipment is conditional upon the conformity of the L/C with our Sales Confirmation.

We hope that in future you will establish the Letters of Credit exactly according to the terms and conditions of relevant Sales Confirmation, or include in them such terms as "AS PER S/C No…"

By so doing you will not only save much trouble, but also help to facilitate shipment of your products.

We are awaiting your bank's credit amendment.

Best Wishes.

Sincerely

Helen chen

Manager

Helen Chen

Manager of Sales Department

National Silk Corp.,

Add: No.12 Heping Road, Heping Dist., Tianjin, China

Tel: +86 022 23564452

Fax: +86 022 23564455

8.3.4 Letter Four

(Asking for Extension of the L/C)

Kee & Co., Ltd.

34 Regent Street, London, UK

10 Feb., 2018

National Silk Corporation

Tianjin, China

Dear Ms. Mary，

We thank you for your L/C for the captioned goods. We are regretful that owing to some delay on the part of our suppliers at the point of origin, we are not able to get the goods ready before the end of this month. As a result, we sent you a cable yesterday reading: L/C NW1415 PLS CABLE EXTENSION SHIPMENT VALIDITY 15/31 MAY RESPECTIVELY LETFOLLOWS.

It is expected that the consignment will be ready for shipment in the early part of May and we are arranging to ship it on s/s "Haihang" sailing from Tianjin on or about 10 May.

We are looking forward to receiving your bank's extension of the above L/C thus enabling us to effect shipment of the goods in question.

Your cooperation in this respect will be appreciated.

Sincerely,

Porter Erisman

Vice-President

8.3.5 Letter Five

(Accepting the L/C Amendment)

Kee & Co., Ltd.
34 Regent Street, London, UK

15 Feb., 2018

National Silk Corp.
Add: No.12 Heping Road, Heping Dist., Tianjin, China
Tel: +86 022 23564452
Fax: +86 022 23564455

Dear Ms. Helen,

We have received your letter asking for amendment to the L/C No.NEW-BALCA05. We are sorry to learn that the L/C contains several discrepancies. Anyhow, after careful study of your letter, we are now informing you that we have instructed our banker to amend the L/C accordingly.

We think you will receive the L/C Amendment in due time. We trust that everything is now in order and you will be able to ship the goods in time.

We are looking forward to receiving your shipping advice.

Yours sincerely,
Kee & Co., Ltd.
Manager
John Smith

8.3.6　Letter Six

NOTIFICATION OF AMENDMENT

BANK OF CHINA

BANK OF CHINA JIANGSU BRANCH
ADDRESS: 148 ZHONGSHAN SOUTH ROAD NANJING

CABLE CHUNGKUO TELEX: 34116/34127 BOCJS CN SWIFT: BKCHCNBJ940 FAX: 4208843	NOTIFICATION OF AMENDMENT	
		2018/04/09
		AD94001A40576
TO 致：0000660	WHEN CORRESPOND NG	

ZHEJIANG CATHAYA INTL CO.,LTD. 117 TIYUCHANG ROAD, HANGZHOU, CHINA FAX:0571-85199159	PLEASE QUOTE OUT REF NO.	
ISSUING BANK 开证行 800333 ALRAJHI BANKING AND INVESTMENT CORPORATION RIYADH	TRANSMITTED TO US THROUGH 　转递行 REF NO.	

L/C NO.信用证号	DATED 开证日期	AMOUNT 金额	EXPIRY PLACE 有效地
0011LC123756	2018/04/05	USD13,260.00	FOREIGN
EXPIRY DATE 有效期	TENOR 期限	CHARGE 未付费用	CHARGE BY 费用承担人
2018/05/25	SIGHT	RMB0.00	BENE
RECEIVED VIA 来证方式	AVAILABLE 是否生效	TEST/SIGN 印押是否相符	CONFIRM 我行是否保兑
SWIFT	VALID	YES	NO

DEAR SIRS敬启者：

WE HAVE PLEASURE IN ADVISING YOU THAT WE HAVE RECEIVED FROM THE A/M BANK A(N) AMENDMENT TO THE CAPTIONED L/C, CONTENTS OF WHICH ARE AS PER ATTACHED SHEET(S).

THIS AMENDMENT SHOULD BE ATTACHED TO THE CAPTIONED L/C ADVISED BY US, OTHERWISE, THE BENEFICIARY WILL BE RESPONSIBLE FOR ANY CONSEQUENCES ARISING THEREFROM.

REMARK备注：

THIS AMENDMENT CONSISTS OF_____ SHEET(S), INCLUDING THE COVERING LETTER AND ATTACHMENT(S).

KINDLY TAKE NOTE THAT THE PARTIAL ACCEPTANCE OF THE AMENDMENT IS NOT ALLOWED.

THIS AMENDMENT IS ADVISED SUBJECT TO LCC UCP PUBLICATION WHICH APPLY TO THE ORIGINAL L/C.

YOURS FAITHFULLY,
BANK OF CHINA

AMENDMENT TO A DOCUMENTARY CREDIT

2018 JUL 17 14:02:28	LOGICAL TERMINAL H020
MTS707	AMENDMENT TO A DOCUMENTARY CREDIT

PAGE 00001

FUNC MSG700

UMR 41710126

MSGACK DWS765I AUTH OK, KEY DIGEST, BKCHCNBJ BOTKJPJT RECORO	
BASIC HEADER	F 01 BKCHCNBJA910 1778 261570
APPLICATION HEADER	0 707 1328 140717 BOTKJPJTAOSA 1584 815346 140717 1228 N * BANK OF TOKYO-MITSUBISHI UFJ, LTD. * THE OSAKA
USER HEADER	SERVICE CODE 103: BANK. PRIORITY 113: MSG USER REF. 108: INFO. FROM CI 115:

SENDER'S REF.	* 20 :	S-441-2000029
RECEIVER'S REF.	* 21 :	NON REF.
DATE OF ISSUE	31 C:	180430
DATE OF AMENDMENT	30 :	180717
NUMBER OF AMENDMENT	26 E:	01
BENEFICIARY	* 59 :	ZHEJIANG CATHAYA INTERNATIONAL CO., LTD. 117 TIYUCHANG ROAD,HANGZHOU,CHINA
NEW DATE OF EXPIRY	31 E:	181015
INCREASE DOC.CREDIT	32 B:	CURRENCY USD AMOUNT 23,000.00
NEW AMOUNT	34 B:	CURRENCY USD AMOUNT 55,000.00
POS./NEG.TOL.(%)	39 A:	10/10
LATEST SHIPMENT	44 C:	180924
TRAILER:		ORDER IS <MAC:> <PAC:> <ENC:> <CHK:> <TNG:> <PDE:> MAC:F02FD807 CHK:B81919F459DB

8.4 Words and Phrases

1. **agreed-upon**   *adj.*   constituted or contracted by stipulation or agreement   同意；商定

e.g.   Contract is worth nothing if the event does not take place in the agreed-upon period of time.

2. **catalyst**   *n.*   something that causes an important event to happen   催化剂

e.g.   The First World War served as a catalyst for major social changes in Europe.

3. credit-worthiness　*n.*　trustworthiness with money as based on a person's credit history　资信状况

e.g.　The conventional banks give greater emphasis on credit-worthiness of the clients.

4. go through　浏览；检查

e.g.　Go through the text from the beginning.

5. discrepancy　*n.*　a difference between conflicting facts or claims or opinions　不符点；差异

e.g.　In case documents presented with discrepancies, a discrepancy fee of USD 15.00 will be charged.

6. set forth　*vt.*　陈述（陈列；出发；宣布）

e.g.　Please follow the terms and conditions set forth in our S/C No. 123.

7. in full conformity with　和……完全相符

e.g.　The stipulations of your L/C should be in full conformity with those of the S/C.

8. countersign　*v.*　add one's signature to after another's to attest authenticity　副署；会签

e.g.　You must countersign on this line of the contract.

9. instruct　*v.*　impart skills or knowledge to, teach, learn　教授；指导

e.g.　He instructed me in building a boat.

　　　　　　　v.　give instructions or directions for some task　指示；命令

e.g.　She instructed the students to work on their pronunciation

10. turn out to be　be shown or be found to be　结果是

e.g.　A loss may turn out to be a gain.

11. regular　*adj.*　in accordance with fixed order or procedure or principle　定期的；有规律的

e.g.　regular orders; his regular calls on his customers; regular meals

12. in the near future　最近；不久

e.g.　See you again in the near future. 后会有期！

13. approach　*v.*　come near in time　接近

e.g.　Winter is approaching.

14. recall　*v.*　think back　回想起；召回；恢复

e.g.　He could recall her face fairly.

15. turn for the better　好转

e.g.　Things will probably take a turn for the better soon.

16. point out　指出；解释

e.g.　I beg to point out that your facts are incorrect.

17. take effective measures　采取有效措施

e.g.　The government should take effective measures to solve the possible problems of Holiday Economy, so this new economy will have smooth development.

18. occurrence　*n.*　an event that happens　事件；发生

e.g.　Signing contracts is a common occurrence in foreign trade.

19. **do your utmost**　尽全力

e.g.　We are wholeheartedly welcomed domestic and overseas customers' inquiry, we will do our utmost to serve you.

20. **expedite**　*v.*　speed up the progress of; facilitate　加快；促进

e.g.　Please do your utmost to expedite the covering L/C, so that we may execute the order smoothly.

21. **accordingly**　*adv.*　in accordance with　因此；于是；相应地

e.g.　We have made modification to your L/C accordingly.

22. **enter into**　参加；建立

e.g.　We wish to enter into business relations with your company.

23. **assortment**　*n.*　the act of distributing things into classes or categories of the same type　分类

e.g.　The shop has a rich assortment of goods.

24. **respectively**　*adv.*　in the order given　各自地；分别地

e.g.　The brothers were called Felix and Max, respectively.

8.5　Notes

1. **On receiving the L/C, the beneficiary will check the terms and conditions against the Sales Contract to ensure that everything agrees with the credit requirement.**　一收到信用证，受益人就会审查其条款是否与合同相符，以确保一切都符合信用证的要求。

agree with　与……相一致

e.g.　Saying and doing should agree with each other.

2. **In such a case, the exporter is obliged to urge the importer to establish the L/C in time in order not to delay shipment.**　此种情况下，出口商不得不催促进口商及时开立信用证，以确保不延期装运。

in such a case　在此种情况下

e.g.　Keeping silent in such a case amounts to supporting the speaker.

oblige　*v.*　force or compel somebody to do something　强迫；强制

oblige sb. to do sth.　强迫某人做某事

e.g.　It must be noted that the bank is obliged to make payment even though the buyer may default.

3. **put this step in an important position**　将这一步放在一个重要的位置上

e.g.　It is extremely essential to put education development in an important position.

4. **a minor difference**　微小的差异

5. **soft clause**　软条款

6. **With reference to**　关于；根据

e.g.　With reference to our representative's call, we are pleased to say that we have obtained the receipt for the goods.

7. **We should have refused then to effect shipment, but we acceded to your request for fulfillment of your order.**　我方应该拒绝交货，但我方仍同意按照你方的要求完成订单。

effect shipment　发运货物；交货

e.g.　Please be assured that we will effect shipment according to the contracted terms.

accede to　同意；答应

e.g.　Will you accede to her request?

8. **have no alternative but to cancel the contract**　除了取消合同别无选择

have no alternative but to do　除了……别无选择

e.g.　Since your price is too high to be acceptable we have no alternative but to place our order elsewhere.

9. **cause us much inconvenience**　引起诸多不便

e.g.　I certainly didn't intend to cause you so much inconvenience.

10. **transshipment prohibited**　禁止转运

11. **in no way to blame**　决不责怪

　　in no way to　决不

e.g.　Such discrepancies are in no way to be considered a criterion for our future supplies.

12. **in two equal monthly lots**　分两个月等量

　　in a single lot　一批

e.g.　We are pleased to say that we are agreeable to your request for shipment in two equal monthly lots.

13. **facilitate shipment of your products**　方便/有助于产品的运输

　　facilitate　*v.*　make easier　帮助；使……容易；促进

e.g.　You could facilitate the process by sharing your knowledge.

14. **s/s**　*n.*　**steamship**（缩）轮船

15. **shipping advice**　装运通知；发货通知

e.g.　Immediately upon receipt of shipping advice, we will send the shipping documents through the Bank of China, Tianjin.

8.6　Useful Expressions

1. In order to avoid amendment in future, please make sure that the clauses of the L/C are in accordance with those of contract.

为了避免今后改证，请确保信用证内容与合同一致。

2. We have received your L/C NO.1236 issued by the Mercantile Bank, New York for the

amount of US$25,300 covering 30,000 dozen Stretch Nylon Socks.

我们已收到纽约商业银行开立的金额为 25 300 美元的第 1236 号信用证，以支付 30 000 打弹性尼龙袜。

3. In spite of our repeated requests, we still have not received your Letter of Credit up to now, thus entailing unnecessary delay and expenses. Please open the credit immediately, otherwise, we cannot effect shipment as scheduled.

尽管再三催请开证，仍未收到你方信用证，从而导致了不必要的延迟和增加了额外的费用。请立即开立信用证，否则我方无法按计划交货。

4. It is to be pointed out that the goods under our S/C No.112 (Your Order No.4831) have been ready for quite some time and we have been waiting for your L/C; however to our regret, we haven't received it and heard anything from you.

我们想指出，我方第 112 号售货确认书（你方第 4381 号订单）项下的货物备妥待运已久。我方一直在等待你方的信用证，但是令我们遗憾的是，我们既没有收到信用证也没有收到任何信息。

5. We are pleased to inform you that we have been requested to open a confirmed and irrevocable Letter of Credit in your favor.

我们很高兴地通知您，我方将开立以贵方为受益人的保兑的不可撤销信用证。

6. We would like you to instruct your bank to authorize their correspondent bank to confirm the L/C when advising us of the same.

我方希望贵方通知你方银行授权其在我处的代理行在向我们通知信用证时予以保兑。

7. The terms of payment are by Confirmed, Irrevocable Letter of Credit in our favor, available by Draft at Sight, reaching us one month ahead of shipment, remaining valid for negotiation in China for another 21 days after the prescribed time of shipment, and allowing transshipment and partial shipments.

付款条件是保兑的、不可撤销的信用证，凭即期汇票付款，信用证应在装运前一个月寄达我处，在规定的装运日期后 21 天内在中国议付有效，允许转船和分批装运。

8. We shall open through a bank an Irrevocable Sight Letter of Credit to reach you 10 days before the month of shipment, stipulating that 50% of the invoice value available against clean draft at sight while the remaining 50% on Documents against Payment at sight on collection basis.

我们将通过银行开立不可撤销的即期信用证，在装运日期前 10 天内到达你处，信用证全额为发票金额的 50%，以即期光票支付，其余 50%货款在托收方式下即期付款交单。

9. The requesting party shall bear the bank charges for the amendment to or extension of Letters of Credit as and when such situations arise.

如果需要改证或展证，提出的一方将承担有关的银行费用。

10. Since there is no direct steamer sailing for your port, we would request you to amend your L/C to allow transshipment.

由于没有驶往你方港口的直达船，我方要求你方将信用证修改为允许转船。

8.7　Exercises

1. Answer the following questions.

(1) Detail the whole process of how to open a Letter of Credit.

(2) As the importer fails to open the credit, what should the exporter do?

(3) How do the discrepancies influence the exporter and the importer?

(4) Why is it important to go through all the clauses set forth in the L/C, after receiving the Letter of Credit?

(5) What is the usual process for the buyer to require amendment to an L/C? And what about the seller?

(6) Why should clauses be paid special attention, when amendment is needed?

2. Discuss on the following topic.

In China, the term of payment by L/C are the most usual mode, for payment by L/C can give the best protection to the exporters. However, it will not benefit the foreign importer. Discuss how a seller could persuade the buyer to accept payment by L/C.

3. Write a letter.

You have received a letter of the exporter, Kee & Co., Ltd., who wants to extend the L/C NW1415 to the 31 of May and the 15 of June for shipment and negotiation respectively. Write a reply to the letter, tell the exporter that due to the complicated formalities of applying for licenses and its validity, you cannot extend the relevant L/C.

4. Translate the following sentences into English.

（1）我方的付款要求是凭附带全套已装船单据的即期汇票开立的信用证，在装货港所在地银行议付。

（2）第 126 号合约项下的 800 公吨钢管已备妥待运，但至今我们尚未收到你方的相关信用证。请速开来以免证误装运期。

（3）你方须在 2018 年 3 月 20 日前开出信用证，否则，我方保留撤销合同的权利，不另行通知。

（4）很抱歉在此种情况下我们不得不请求将该信用证的装运期和交单期分别延期至 8 月 31 日和 9 月 15 日。

（5）我们已收到有关信用证，但发现以下不符点。

（6）我们的合同规定本次交易允许的佣金应是 3%且允许分批装运，但我方发现信用证上要求 4%的佣金且注明禁止分批装运，因此，请你方通知银行修改信用证。

（7）既然贵方坚持，我方将修改信用证。由此产生的后果，由你方自行承担。

5. Translate the following passage into Chinese.

(1) Normally, the Credit will be "irrevocable", that is once it has been received by or advised to the beneficiary it can't be retracted or changed without the beneficiary's consent, and the opening bank must meet any drafts presented provided the terms of the Letter of Credit have been complied with.

(2) If we give notice of refusal of documents presented under this credit, we shall however retain the right to accept a waiver of discrepancies from the applicant and, subject to such wavier being acceptable to us, to release documents against that waiver without reference to the presenter provided that no written instructions to the contrary have been received by us from the presenter before the release, instructions shall not constitute a failure on our part to hold the documents at the presenter's risk and disposal, and we will have no liability to the presenter in respect of any such release.

(3) We request you to have L/C No.165 amended as follows：

① extend the time of shipment till June 27；

② extend the validity of the L/C till July 24.

Await your amendment advice.

(4) Please amend by fax L/C No.165 as allowing transshipment and partial shipment.

(5) Owing to the late arrival of the steamer on which we have booked space, we would appreciate you extending the shipment date and validity of your L/C No.148 to 29 March and 14 April respectively.

Specimen L/C (by SWIFT)

TO: BANK OF CHINA, TIANJIN BRANCH
DATE: 12 JUNE, 2018.

Sequence of Total:	*27: 1/3
Form of Doc. Credit:	*40 A: IRREVOCABLE/TRANSFERABLE
Doc. Credit Number:	*20: L10394
Date of Issue:	*31 C: 20180612
Date and Place of Expiry :	*31 D: 20180715 IN CHINA
Issuing Bank:	52 A: CRITITM
	CREDITO ITALIANO S.P.A.
	LUMEZZANE
	ITALY
Applicant:	*50: SALTMAN EST.
	VIA UNITE OF ITALIA，28
	24 CALUSCO（BG）

ITALY

Beneficiary:	*59: TIANJIN GARMENTS IMPORT AND EXPORT CORP.,
	NO. 1 YOU YI ROAD, HEXI DISTRICT,
	TIANJIN, CHINA
Currency Code, Amount:	*32 B: USD53, 052.00
	NOT EXCEEDING
Available with/by:	*41 D: ANY BANK BY NEGOTIATION
Drafts at:	*42 C: 60 DAYS AFTER SIGHT
Drawee:	*42 D: ISTITUTO BANCARTO SAN PAOLO DI
	TORINO S.P.A.
	LECCO
Partial Shipment:	*43 P: PROHIBITED
Transshipment:	*43 T: PERMITTED
Loading in Charge:	*44 A: ANY CHINESE PORT
For Transport to	*44 B: GENOVA ITALY
Latest date of Shipment:	*44 C: 20180630
Description of Goods:	*45 A:

WATER REPELLENT JACKET AND PANT SETS,

UNDER CONTRACT NO. TG2003034 (TOTAL 1,080 SETS)

EACH SET PACKING IN PLASTIC BAG, 12 SET PER CARTON. CFR GENOVA

SAMPLE NO. A8004:   STYLE No. MC5 20DOZS AT USD35.5/SET

No. MD5 22DOZS AT USD40.5/SET

SAMPLE NO. A8007:   No. MC5 20DOZS AT USD50/SET

No. MD5 28DOZS AT USD65/SET

----------------------------SWIFT 701-------------------------------------

Sequence of Total:	*27: 2/3
Doc. Credit Number:	*21: L10394
Documents required:	*46 A:

1 – COMMERCIAL INVOICE IN QUADRUPLICATE GIVING FULL

DESCRIPTIONS OF EACH GARMENT AND INDICATING

STYLES NUMBER

2 – CERTIFICATE OF ORIGIN IN 2 COPIES INDICATING THIS CREDIT NO.

3 – PACKING LIST IN TRIPLICATE INDICATING STYLE NO., DETAILS

OF PACKING, GROSS WEIGHT, NET WEIGHT, AND DIMENSIONS OF

EACH CARTON AND CERTIFYING THAT ALL WEIGHTS AND

MEASUREMENTS ARE IN MEYRIC SYSTEM AND BUYER'S

SAMPLES NUMBERS APPEAR ON ALL CARTONS

4 – FULL SET ORIGINAL OF CLEAN ON BOARD OCEAN BILL OF LADING ISSUED TO ORDER AND MARKED FREIGHT PAID WITH NOTIFYING APPLICANT, INDICATING THIS L/C NUMBER AND EVIDENCING SHIPMENT VIA AMERICAN PRESIDENT LINE OR SEA LINE.

5 – THE COPY OF THE TELEX SENT DIRECTLY TO APPLICANT WITHIN 2 DAYS AFTER SHIPMENT INDICATING THE SHIPMENT DETAILS AS FOLLOWS:

THE VESSEL NAME, VOYAGE NO.;

BILL OF LADING NO. AND DATE;

DESCRIPTION OF GOODS;

QUANTITIES AND AMOUNT.

CHARGES: *71 B:

ALL BANKING CHARGES OTHER THAN OUR OWN ARE FOR BENEFICIARY'S ACCOUNT

PERIOD FOR PRESENTATION: *48:

+DOCUMENTS MUST BE PRESENTED FOR NEGOTIATION WITHIN 15 DAYS FROM THE DATE OF SHIPMENT BUT NO LATER THAN THE EXPIRATION DATE. CONFIRMATION INSTRUCTIONS:*49: WITHOUT

INSTRUCTIONS TO THE PAY/ACC/NEG BANK:*78 :

+A FEE OF USD75 WILL BE IMPOSED ON EACH SET OF DOC. RECEIVED BY US CONTAINING ANY DISCREPACIES UNDER THIS CREDIT.

+THIS LETTER OF CREDIT IS TRANSFERABLE.WE WILL HONOR DRAFTS DRAWN BY DRAWERS IN COMPLIANCE WITH THIS CREDIT TERMS. THE NEGOTIATING BANK MUST CERTIFY ON COVER LETTER OF SAID DOCUMENTS REVERSE SIDE OF THE ORIGINAL LETTER OF CREDIT.

SENDER TO RECEIVER INFORMATION: *72:

THIS CREDIT IS SUBJECT TO UNIFORM CUSTOMS AND PRACTICE FOR DOCUMENTARY CREDITS 600

--------------------------SWIFT 701-------------------------------------

Sequence of Total: *27: 3/3

Doc. Credit Number: *40 B: L10394

Additional Conditions: *47 A:

–ALL DOCUMENTS MUST INDICATE THIS CREDIT NUMBER.

–NEGOTIATION BANK MUST FORWARD ALL DOCUMENTS TO US AT OUR COUNTERS LOCATED AT XXX.

–IN CASE OF TRANSFER, A THROUGH BILL OF LADING IS ACCEPTABLE.

–BUYER'S SAMPLE NUMBER MUST APPER ON ALL DOCUMENTS.

–TRANSFERS UNDER THIS CREDIT ARE PROHIBITED TO PERSONS IN THE

FOLLOWING COUNTRIES: NORTH KOREA, CUBA, LIBYA, IRAN AND IRAQ.

BEST REGARDS,
R07046
23233 TJBOC CN

Answers for Reference

Chapter 9   Packing and Shipping Mark

9.1   Introduction

9.1.1   Packing

The packing clause is a necessary term in an Imp. & Exp. contract. It's a very important section of goods instruction. The exporter shall make delivery in exact accordance with the requests of packaging set forth in the contract.

Generally speaking, in international trade, there are two kinds of packing: transport packing and sales packing.

First, Transport packing is also called large packing or outer packing. On one hand, transport packing can protect the goods from being damaged. On the other hand, proper transport packing is good for handling and long distance transportation.

Second, sales packing is also called small packing or inner packing. It refers to the initial packing. It can also protect the product. In addition, good sales packing can beautify the goods in order to attract the customers' attention and give them a deep impression.

Normal packings are as follows: wooden case, iron case, crate, carton, wooden drum, iron drum, plastic drum, bale, cloth bag, gunny bag, paper bag, plastic bag, cylinder, flask, jar, box, basket, can, tin, pallet, container, etc.

In recent years, there are lots of Green Trade Barriers. Most of them require green packing, so packing materials must not only protect the goods in transportation, but also can be helpful to environmental protection.

9.1.2   Shipping Mark

Shipping Mark is printed on the outer packing. It contains the information such as product name, country of origin, consignee, port of destination, weight, package number, and so on.

On the outer packing, you may also find warning mark and indicative mark. They both inform the carrier or the customer to handle the goods with special care. Familiar warning mark and indicative mark are as follows:

NO HOOK	NO SMOKING
AWAY FROM HEAT	STOW AWAY FROM BOILER
OPEN HERE	PERISHABLE
HANDLE WITH CARE	THIS SIDE UP
INFLAMMABLE	EXPLOSIVE
FRAGILE	FUSIBLE
ACID-WITH CARE	GLASS-WITH CARE

9.2　Writing Guide

When a buyer writes a packing letter, three parts are included.

At the beginning, you should show that this letter is about packing. In the second place, buyers can give some detailed packing instructions such as the packing material, shipping mark, packing design and so forth. Third, show your appreciation and hope.

When a seller replies to the letter, he can also propose some suggestions about the packing. For example, he can talk about the packing material and the colors of the packing. He would better describe his idea particularly.

9.3　Letters for Example

9.3.1　Letter One

(Packing Requirements)

FANGZHENG CULTURE IMPORT & EXPORT CORP.

235 Wuyi Street

SHANGHAI,CHINA

Telephone No: …

E-Mail Address:fzcie_corp@ fzcie.com

Fax: …

April 12,2018

KING CORP.

124 Manor Street

Los Angeles, USA

Dear Sirs,

Thank you for your letter of April 10,2018.We are pleased to inform you the packing of

---

the goods ordered by you is as follows:

The books under captioned contract should be wrapped in waterproof bags, 100 books per bag and 10 bags are packed in a wooden case. This kind of packing is waterproof and is well protected against moisture. It is fairly fit for ocean transportation and strong enough to stand rough handling. You can be rest assured that this kind of packing is seaworthy enough for the safe arrival of the goods at your destination.

Looking forward to your early reply.

Yours faithfully,

LiHua

Manager

9.3.2 Letter Two

(Asking for Improving Packing)

KING CORP.

124 Manor Street

LOS ANGELES,USA

Telephone No: …

E-Mail Address:king_corp@ king.com

Fax: …

April 17,2018

Fangzhang Culture Import & Export Corp.

235 Wuyi Street

Shanghai

China

Dear Mr Li,

We have received your letter of April 12 with pleasure. Totally speaking, your suggestion about packing is very good. But we believe wooden case is not necessary because it's too heavy.

We believe waterproof carton is a better choice since cartons are comparatively light and compact, which are more convenient to handle in loading and unloading. Besides, these cartons are well protected against moisture by plastic lining. In view of the above reasons , you can use cartons to instead. Each carton contains 10 bags.

We hope you will accept our suggestion and appreciate your cooperation.

Yours faithfully,

Henry Smith

President

9.3.3　Letter Three

(Shipping Marks Requirements)

SANDY WOOD CO., LTD.

P.O.BOX 123

88 Peral Road

MANCHESTER, ENGLAND

TEL: …

E-Mail:sandywood_corp@ sandywood.com

Fax: …

May 3, 2018

Tianjin International Imp. & Exp Co., Ltd.

25 Zhujiang Street

Tianjin, China

Dear Mr Ford,

　　Re: Sales Confirmation No.198

　　We are now writing to you in regard to the packing of the cargo of chinaware, which we feel necessary to clarify for our future dealings.

　　As chinaware is susceptible to be broken, we would like hard foamed plastic padding for each and wooden cases outside capable of withstanding rough handling. In addition, please remember to stencil warning markings such as "FRAGILE", "HANDLE WITH CARE" on the wooden cases. We hope you pay special attention to the packing.

　　Please let us know whether these requirements could be met. Your early response will be appreciated.

Yours faithfully,

Zhu Gui

Manager

9.3.4　Letter Four

(Sales Packing Requirement)

TIANJIN INTERNATIONAL IMP. & EXP. CO., LTD.

25 Zhujiang Street

TIANJIN, CHINA

TEL: …

E-Mail:tjiie_cl@tjiiecl.com

Fax: …

February 8,2018

Sandy Wood Co., Ltd.

P.O.BOX 123

88 Peral Road

Manchester, England

Dear Mr Zhu,

　　We thank you for your email dated February 3, and wish to inform you as follows:

　　The sales packing must be attractive and helpful to the sales, because one important function of sales packing is to stimulate the buyer's desire to buy. It is helpful that customers fall in love with your product at the first sight. You can change the color and the shape. We hope you will be able to send us your improved designs in two weeks.

　　We trust that the requirements are clear to you and your full cooperation is appreciated.

Yours sincerely,

Henry Ford

President

9.4　Words and Phrases

　　1. **cargo**　*n.*　the things which are taken from one place to another in a ship, plane, or other vehicle　货物

　　2. **clarify**　*v.*　to make something easier to understand by explaining it more fully　澄清

　　3. **dealing**　*n.*　transactions or relations with others, usually in business　行为；交易

　　4. **fragile**　*adj.*　easily broken, damaged, or destroyed　易碎的

　　5. **mark**　*n.*　a sign, such as a cross, made in lieu of a signature　标志

　　6. **moisture**　*n.*　the state or quality of being damp　潮湿；湿气

　　7. **pack**　*v.*　to put things into a case or other container　包装

　　8. **packing**　*n.*　material used in packing　包装；包装材料；包装方法

　　9. **padding**　*n.*　material used to pad something　填料

　　10. **seaworthy**　*adj.*　in good condition and fit for a sea voyage　适于航海的；经得起航海的

　　11. **stencil**　*v.*　to print by using a templet　印上模板图案或字样

　　12. **susceptible**　*adj.*　yielding readily to or capable of　易受……的

　　13. **waterproof**　*adj.*　impervious to or unaffected by water　防水的

14. **wrap**   *v.*   to put something around something else to cover or protect it   包好；裹住
15. **in addition**   over and above; besides   除此之外
16. **inform sb. sth**.   to tell sb. sth.   通知某人某事

9.5   Notes

1. 部分常用的出口包装容器名称：

bag   袋；包   **gunny bag**   麻袋   **poly bag**   塑料袋

bale   包；布包   **box**   盒；桶   **bundle**   捆

carton   纸箱   **case**   箱   **wooden case**   木箱

cask   木桶   **keg**   小圆桶   **drum**   铁皮圆桶

pallet   托盘；小货盘   **container**   集装箱

2. **shipping mark**   唛头

indicative mark   指示性标记

e.g.

Keep Cool   保持凉爽   Keep Flat   平放   Keep Dry   保持干燥

Keep Upright   直放   This Side Up   此端向上   Open This End   此端开启

warning mark   警告性标记

e.g.

Poison   有毒   Dangerous Goods   危险物品

On Deck   置于甲板   Fragile   易碎

Don't Throw Down   不可投掷   Handle With Care   小心搬运

No Hooks   不准用钩   Away From Heat   远离热源

Glass With Care   小心玻璃   Acid-With Care   酸性品

Inflammable   易燃物品

3. **consignee**   收件人；收货人

   consigner   发货人

4. **net weight**   净重

   gross weight   毛重

   tare weight   皮重

5. **You can be rest assured that this kind of packing is seaworthy enough for the safe arrival of the goods at your destination.**   请你方放心，这种包装很适合海运，货物将安全抵达你方目的地。

6. **…one important function of sales packing is to stimulate the buyer's desire to buy.**   销售包装的一个重要功能在于它能够刺激消费者的购买欲望。

9.6 Useful Expressions

1. The packing of this article features novel design and diversified styles.
该产品的包装特点是设计新颖，形式多样。

2. Packed in veneer cases of 25kg net each, lined with wax or parchment paper, wire strapped.
表面镶板箱包装，每箱净重二十五公斤，内衬蜡纸或硫酸纸，外加铁腰子。

3. The inner packing must be attractive and helpful to the sales.
内包装必须具有吸引力，这样有利于销售。

4. The goods are to be packed in wooden cases containing 20 dozen each.
货物用木箱包装，每箱 20 打。

5. The packing must be seaworthy and strong enough to stand rough handling.
包装必须适合海运，足够牢固，经得住野蛮搬运。

6. No name of country or trademark is to appear on the outside containers.
外箱上不得出现国名和商标。

7. We must make it clear that with the different packing material, the packing expenses will be different.
我们必须说清楚：采用不同的包装材料，包装费会不一样。

8. Because the goods will be transshipped, I hope each case will be marked with details of weight, warning symbols and directions, as well as your own marks.
由于货物要转船，所以我希望每个箱体上标注重量说明、警告性标志、指示性标志及你方自己的标志。

9. Please remember to stencil "KEEP DRY" "DO NOT TURN OVER" and other necessary marks on the cartons.
请记住在纸箱上涂刷"保持干燥""请勿翻转"及其他必要的标记。

10. Our packing will prove satisfactory in every respect to your customers.
我方包装将在各方面令你方客户满意。

11. We give you on the attached sheet full details regarding packing and marking. These must be strictly observed.
我们随信寄去的附件上写明了所有关于包装和唛头的详细要求。请严格遵守这些要求。

9.7 Exercises

1. Choose the best answer.

(1) _____ please finds our price list.

　　A. Enclose　　　　　B. Enclosed　　　　　C. Enclosing　　　　D. Be enclosed

(2) We don't know that canned goods _____ the scope of your business activities.

    A. meet   B. fall within   C. reach   D. get into

(3) Type 1 is _____ , so its price is considerably higher than that of last year.

    A. in short supply   B. in free supply   C. out of supply   D. for supply

(4) Pens are packed 12 pieces _____ a box and 200 boxes _____ a wooden cases.

    A. to, in   B. in, to   C. to, to   D. to, of

(5) We would suggest that you _____ the carton with double straps.

    A. will secure   B. securing   C. secure   D. are secured

(6) Packing charges _____ in the price, and we can make delivery whenever you wish.

    A. in included   B. are included   C. include   D. included

(7) This container can be easily opened _____ both ends.

    A. by   B. on   C. at   D. in

(8) We are confident that the package of our products will _____ the roughest handing in transit.

    A. stand up to   B. stand to   C. suffer from   D. put up

(9) The overall _____ of the case are 100cm ×50cm×50cm.

    A. volumes   B. weights   C. capacities   D. dimensions

(10) It was found upon examination that nearly 20% of the _____ has been broken, obviously due to improper_____.

    A. packing, packages   B. packages, packing

    C. packing, packing   D. packages, packages

2. Translate the following sentences into English.

（1）我们想把纸板箱包装改为木箱包装。

（2）请用金属条加固这种纸板箱。

（3）包装时请考虑下面两种情形：这些盒子很可能遭遇野蛮装卸；它们必须能承受在糟糕的路面上运输。

（4）水泥要用双层牛皮纸袋包装，每袋装 50 公斤。

（5）这种又轻又结实的箱子能节约舱位，并且便于储存和分拨货物。

（6）跟以前一样，箱子上要刷制一个菱形标志，内写我公司的首字母。

（7）我们的包装方式已经被其他客户广泛接受，到目前为止还没有收到任何投诉。

（8）请在外包装上标明"小心轻放"字样。

（9）为了减少包装费用，我们打算采用可重复使用的材料来包装货物。

（10）请严格遵守包装及标记的细则。

3. Translate the following sentences into Chinese.

(1) When you packed, please put 2 or 3 different designs and colors in each box.

(2) We can meet your requirements to have the goods packed in wooden cases but you have

to bear the extra packing charge.

(3) Quality is essential in business transactions, but packing can't be neglected in the least because good packing contributes greatly to the sale.

(4) Actually, this packing is both shockproof and moisture proof. Nevertheless we have still marked the cartons with warnings like "FRAGILE" "USE NO HOOK" and "DO NOT DROP".

(5) All the cartons are lined with plastic sheets, so they're absolutely waterproof, I can assure you.

(6) The continued increases in freight costs force us to seek improved packing methods. Could you suggest a more economical packing method for our products?

(7) The fruit jam under the captioned should be packed in tinplate cans of 400ml each in weight, with 46 cans in a wooden case.

(8) Chemical foaming represents a new method in the field of packing. Enclosed please find a brochure from which you will learn more about the possibilities of application.

(9) The Wool Sweater must be packed each in a polythene bag with an inner lining of stout waterproof materials and then in cardboard box, 10 dozen to a carton.

(10) For better results, we now use plastic bags instead of paper ones. This not only gives better protection but adds to the attraction of the goods.

4. Write a letter according to the information given in the following situations, applying the writing principles discussed in this chapter.

（1）感谢买方订购床单。

（2）床单 10 打装一盒，8 盒装一纸箱。

（3）将贵公司名称缩印在菱形内。

（4）将货物生产国名标在纸箱上，而不是每一个盒子上。

（5）将特别提示和警告印在纸箱上。

（6）希望对方对包装满意。

Answers for Reference

Chapter 10   Shipment

10.1   Introduction

In international trade, there are many modes of transportation, such as ocean transportation, air transportation, road transportation and rail way transportation. Ocean transportation is the most used mode of transportation because of its low freight. Basically there are two types of ocean freight according to the assorted shipping vessels used, that is, tramp and liner.

Ocean Bill of Lading is a transport receipt. It is the cargo carrier receipt issued after receipt of the goods and also a proof of shipping contract signed by the carrier. Besides, Ocean Bill of Lading on behalf of the ownership of the goods, is a kind of property rights characteristic of credentials.

Shipment is an indispensable clause in international business contract. Here, shipment refers not only to ocean transportation, but also to road , rail and air transportation. The effectuation of shipment signifies the exporter's fulfillment of the obligation to make delivery of the goods. After the contract is signed the shipment principal should arrange the shipment on time. In fact, shipment operation includes the following procedures: customs declaration, booking shipping space or chartering a ship, making shipment policy, sending shipping advice and so on.

Terms of shipment contains several contents. They are: the time of shipment, the place of shipment, the place of delivery, the place of destination, shipping documents, partial shipment or transshipment.

The time of shipment refers to the time when the cargo is loading on the conveyance. Under FOB, CFR and CIF terms, it's the same as the date on the Bill of Lading.

Before shipment, the importer shall send the exporter a shipping instruction to specify the shipping mark, packing, mode of transportation, etc.

After the goods are loaded on board, the exporter should perform its obligation i.e. sending the shipping advice to importer. Shipping advice includes the contract NO., the name of ship, the name of goods, quantity, value and the time of departure, and so forth.

In some cases, the exporter may choose to deliver a given lot of contracted goods in partial shipment or transshipment. Partial shipment refers that the goods are delivered more than once. Transshipment refers that the direct sailing from the port of loading to the port of destination is unavailable. In the L/C, there should be such statement as "transshipment or partial shipment allowed".

10.2 Writing Guide

1. Shipping Instruction

In writing a shipping instruction, there are three procedures.

First, importer should refer to the contract No. and the terms of trade.

Second, advise some shipping requirements such as the time, document, and so on.

Last, show your hope and some shipping suggestions about cooperation.

2. Shipping Advice

In writing a shipping advice, the seller should give the buyer the following information:

1) Information of the goods

Includes: the name of the goods, S/C number, order number, L/C number, etc.

2) Information of the shipment

Includes: the name of Vessel, estimated time of departure, estimated time of arrival, place of the destination, place of the shipment.

3) Information of the shipping documents

Includes: Bill of Lading, Commercial Invoice, Packing List, Insurance Policy, etc.

10.3 Letters For Example

10.3.1 Letter One

(Shipping Instruction)

TIANJIN INTERNATIONAL IMP. & EXP. CO., LTD.
25 Zhujiang Street
TIANJIN, CHINA
TEL: …
E-Mail:tjiie_cl@tjiiecl.com
Fax: …

March 13, 2018

Mr.Francis Steve
Vice President
Thompson Consumption Group

5... Real Avenue

Sydney, Australia

Dear Mr. Steve,

　　We are glad to receive your letter of March 10, from which we understand that you have booked our order for 500 cartons Niren Zhang craftworks.

　　Our confirmation of the order will be forwarded to you in three days. As our purchase is made on CFR basis, we have arranged shipment with our forwarding agent, SPEED company, Tianjin, who is going to take care of shipping that goods. Once the shipping space is booked, we will inform you the name of the ship. For further instructions, please contact our forwarding agents.

　　We are looking forward to the satisfactory arrival of the goods.

Yours faithfully,

Zhu Gui

Manager

10.3.2　Letter Two

(Urging Shipment)

HUA SHENG IMPORT & EXPORT CORP.

348 Liberation Street

SHANGHAI, CHINA

Telephone No:...

E-Mail Address:hshie_corp@ alibaba.com.cn

Fax: ...

Web sites:www.huashengie.com.cn

September 14, 2018

Snny Electric Company

5... Tang road

Hokkaido, Japan

Dear Sirs,

　　Referring to our previous letters, we would like to remind you that up to now we have not received any news about the shipment.

　　We wish to draw your attention to the contract in caption which stipulates that the shipment is due on September 15 and we should have received your shipping advice by now.

As we have informed you in one of our previous letters, the busy season is drawing near and the users are in urgent need of the goods contracted and are in fact pressing us for assurance of an early delivery. We would like to emphasize that any delay in shipping our booked order will undoubtedly involve us in no small difficulty.

We thank you in advance for your cooperation in this respect and hope you will fax us your shipping advice without further delay.

Yours faithfully,

Hua Sheng

Manager

10.3.3   Letter Three

(Shipping Advice)

TIANJIN INTERNATIONAL IMP. & EXP. CO., LTD.

25 Zhujiang Street

TIANJIN, CHINA

TEL: …

E-Mail:tjiie_cl@tjiiecl.com

Fax: …

October 20, 2018

Mr.Francis Steve

Vice President

Thompson Consumption Group

5… Real Avenue

Sydney, Australia

Dear Mr. Steve,

We are pleased to advise you that we have completed the shipment of your order 0405. The ship is scheduled to sail from Tianjin on October 20 and the estimated time to arrive in Sydney is October 30.We have mailed the documents to you by air this morning. The details are as follows:

Our Contract No. : S123

Your Order No. : O123

Commodity: Niren Zhang craftworks

Quantity : 500 cartons

Invoice Amount : USD35,684.20

Vessel : HERO

B/L No. : V0408

L/C No. : 123456A

Invoice No. : F22345

Insurance Policy No.: BY2564

Packing List No.: CT8524

Shipping Date: October 20, 2018

We trust this consignment will reach you in sound condition and look forward to cooperating with you before long.

Yours faithfully,

Zhu Gui

Manager

10.3.4　Letter Four

(Proposing Partial Shipment)

HUA SHENG IMPORT & EXPORT CORP.

348 Liberation Street

SHANGHAI, CHINA

Telephone No:…

E-Mail Address:hshie_corp@ alibaba.com.cn

Fax: …

Web sites:www.huashengie.com.cn

August 12, 2018

Datai Imp.& Exp. Company

597 Yalu Street

Seoul, Korea

Dear Sir or Madam,

Thank you for your letter of August 10, in which you asked us to advance the shipment of your whole order for bicycle to August 20.

On receiving your letter, we immediately contact the shipping agent. Unfortunately, we are told that there was no enough space for your order during the rest August. If you desire an earlier delivery, the best we can do is to deliver 200 cartons in August and the remainder in September. We hope this arrangement will meet with your approval.

Kindly let us know your opinion as soon as possible.

Yours faithfully,

Hua Sheng

Manager

10.4 Words and Phrases

1. **advance** *v.* to go or move forward or onward 提前

2. **be drawing near = be approaching** 日益临近

3. **confirmation** *n.* the act of confirming 确认

4. **consignment** *n.* a number of goods sent together 托买货物

5. **delivery** *n.* the act of conveying or delivering 交付；交货

6. **forward** *v.* to send letters and parcels to some one's address 发货；寄送

7. **involve sb. in no small difficulty = involve sb. in trouble** 让某人陷入大麻烦

8. **punctual** *adj.* acting or arriving exactly at the time appointed 准时的

9. **remind** *v.* to make someone remember something 提醒

10. **remainder** *n.* something left over after other parts have been taken away 剩余的商品

11. **sound** *adj.* in good condition 情况良好的

12. **steamer** *n.* a vehicle, a machine, or an engine driven by steam 汽船；轮船

13. **stipulate** *v.* to state clearly as a necessary condition of an agreement 规定；保证

14. **urge** *v.* to try very hard to persuade someone to do something 促进；力促；催促

15. **vessel** *n.* a ship or large boat 船舶；轮船

16. **s.s. = steamship** 轮船

17. **Bill of Lading = B/L** a document issued by a carrier to a shipper, listing and acknowledging receipt of goods for transport and specifying terms of 提货单

18. **to be scheduled to =due to** 预计

19. **up to present = up to now** 目前为止

10.5 Notes

1. **shipment** *n.* 装船；装运

gross shipment 总发货量	prompt shipment 立即发货
shipment advice 装运通知	partial shipment 分批装运
date of shipment 发货日期	shipment by installment 分批发运
port of shipment 发运港	suspend shipment 暂停发运

2. **shipping** *n.* 运输

shipping advice 装船通知	shipping documents 运输单据
shipping instruction 装船须知	shipping space 舱位

3. **The users are in urgent need of the goods contracted and are in fact pressing us for assurance of an early delivery.** 客户急需此批货物，并催促我方早日交货。

4. **The ship is scheduled to sail from Tianjin on April 20 and the estimated time to arrive**

in Sydney on is April 30. 该船定于 4 月 20 日从天津启航，预计到达悉尼的时间为 4 月 30 日。

5. **We trust this consignment will reach you in sound condition and look forward to cooperating with you before long.** 我们相信货物会完好无损地抵达贵处，并且期待与你方在不久后再次合作。

10.6　Useful Expressions

1. According to the terms of the contract No.789, shipment is to be effected by the 20 January, and we must have the B/L by the 31 of January at the latest.

按照第 789 号合同，装运事宜应在 1 月 20 日前办理好，提单应当最迟于 1 月 31 日到达我处。

2. Please advise us 30 days before the month of shipment of the contract number, name of commodity, quantity, port of loading and the time when the goods reach the port of loading.

请在交货月份前 30 天将合同号、货名、数量、装运港以及货物到达装运港的时间通知我公司。

3. We are glad to inform you that the goods ordered by you are ready packed for delivery. Shipment can be made immediately after receipt of L/C.

我们高兴地通知贵方，你方订购的货物已备妥待交，一收到信用证就可立即装船。

4. The goods will be ready for shipment by the end of this month. Please inform us the name of the chartered ship and its date of arrival at our port earlier.

货物到本月底可备好等待装运，请尽早通知我方所租船船名及其抵达我港口的日期。

5. Owing to the delayed arrival of the scheduled steamer, we have failed to effect shipment within the L/C validity. Would you please extend the shipment of the L/C for one month, enabling us to proceed with shipment as quickly as possible?

由于预订轮船晚到，我们未能在信用证有效期内完成装运。请你方将信用证的装船期延长一个月，以便我方能尽快着手装船。

6. The shipping space for sailing to London up to the end of this month has been fully booked up.

本月底驶往伦敦的舱位已订满。

7. Much to our regret, we cannot ship the goods within the time limit of the L/C owing to the unforeseen difficulties on the part of mill.

由于出现厂方无法预料的困难，在信用证规定的期限内装运货物已不可能，甚歉。

10.7　Exercises

1. Choose the best answer.

(1) Before shipment, the buyers generally send their _____ to the sellers, informing them

of the packing and marking, mode of transportation,etc.

    A. shipping documents   B. shipping requirements

    C. shipping advice   D. shipping marks

(2) We are very anxious to know when you can definitely _____ shipment.

    A. affect   B. effect   C. carry   D. load

(3) Our advice of dispatch was mailed to you three days ago and you no doubt _____ it by now.

    A. will receive   B. have had received   C. received   D. have received

(4) We look forward to _____ the goods in the fourth quarter.

    A. delivery   B. your delivery   C. deliver   D. the delivery of

(5) _____ any change in the date of delivery, please let us know in advance.

    A. There should be   B. Should there be

    C. There would be   D. Would there be

(6) We regret to say that your price is not _____ the current world market.

    A. on a level with   B. at a level with

    C. in a level with   D. in level with

(7) The goods are urgently needed, we_____ hope you will deliver them immediately.

    A. in the case   B. therefore   C. so   D. for

(8) For all the remaining items the stated dates of delivery are approximate, but _____ caused us certain expenses.

    A. under any circumstances   B. in no case

    C. by all means   D. in any case

(9) Because of the heavy demand _____ the limited supply in the market, it sells fast.

    A. for   B. to   C. from   D. on

(10) If direct steamer is not available for the transportation, _____.

    A. the goods will not be shipped   B. partial shipment should be allowed

    C. the goods have to be separated   D. the goods have to be transshipped

2. Translate the following sentences into English.

（1）该货可以立即交付，准备明日装船。

（2）正如我们在信中所说，客户急需这批货物，我们提议采用分批装运的方式。我们将在5月早些时候将该批货物的1/3先行发运，其余部分将于信用证规定的时期发运。

（3）上述货物已经备好，请早日将装运须知告知我方。

（4）由于以下原因我们停止交货：所需货款尚未支付且你方撤销了购货合同。

（5）我们会按要求将清洁的、已装船、空白抬头提单一式三份交由米兰银行转交你方。

（6）我们的一位客户订购了30 000节干电池，分5批装运，每批数量相等，间隔时间为3个月。

3. Translate the following letter into English.

尊敬的先生：

感谢您 3 月 12 日的来信，你方的信用证号码为 3344。

十分抱歉我方未将你方所订货物装上"成长号"货轮，因为该船已无足够可用舱位。鉴于此，货物将由"玛利亚"号货轮装运，装运时间为本月底。装船一结束，我方将电报你方船名和启航日期。

我们保证将给予你方订货足够的重视，货物将完好无损地交付你方客户，并且期待与你方的进一步合作。

Answers for Reference

Chapter 11   Insurance

11.1   Introduction

In international trade, goods always have a long journey in which it may be destroyed because of various risks, such as bad weather, accidents in loading, unloading, storage, and so on. In order to avoid the losses or damages that might happen, buyers or sellers need to cover insurance on their goods with insurance companies against different risks.

In a contract of insurance, there are two participants: insurer and insured. Insurer refers to the insurance company or underwriter. Insured refers to the buyer or seller. Insured pays the premium to the insurer and then the insured gets a policy which is one of the important documents.

The main clause of insurance includes: coverage, the insurance amount, premium. The risks covered by insurance fall into two categories.

1. The Principle Risks:

(1) F.P.A. (Free from Particular Average)
(2) W.A. (With Average) or W.P.A. (With Particular Average)
(3) All Risks

The buyer or seller covers one of the above the principle risks. If they think it isn't enough, they can also choose "Additional Risks" which include "General Additional Risks" and "Special Additional Risks". Detailed descriptions are as follows.

2. Additional Risks

General Additional Risks:
(1) TPND (Risk of Theft Pilferage and Non-Delivery);
(2) Fresh Water and/or Rain Damage Risk;
(3) Shortage Risk;
(4) Intermixture and Contamination Risk;
(5) Leakage Risk;
(6) Clash and Breakage Risk;
(7) Taint of Odor Risk;
(8) Sweating and Heating Risk;
(9) Hook Damage Risk;

(10) Breakage of Packing Risk.

Special Additional Risks:

(1) War Risk;

(2) Strikes Risk;

(3) Rejection Risk;

(4) On Desk Risk;

(5) Aflatoxin Risk;

(6) Import Duty Risk;

(7) Failure to Deliver Risk.

Generally speaking, the insurance amount is defined as: The total value of the goods based on CIF price+10% of it that is 110% of the total invoice value. If the insured requires more than 110% of the total value, the importer has to bear the additional premium.

When the consignments arrive at the place of destination, inspection firm or organization will inspect the goods. If any damage is found and is to be claimed, insured should submit the insurance policy to the insurer as soon as possible.

11.2　Writing Guide

When writing a letter about insurance, the following information should be considered:

(1) the consignment;

(2) the mode of payment;

(3) the account of insurance;

(4) the coverage of the insurance;

(5) the premium rate;

(6) the way of premium payment;

(7) the validity of the insurance;

(8) the voyage;

(9) insurance company.

11.3　Letters for Example

11.3.1　Letter One

(Asking for Insurance Arrangement)

THOMPSON CONSUMPTION GROUP

5... Real Avenue

SYDNEY, AUSTRALIA

TEL: …

E-Mail:thompson_group@.thompsoncg.com

Fax: …

September 4, 2018

Tianjin International Imp. & Exp. Co.,Ltd.

25 Zhujiang Street

Tianjin, China

Dear Mr. Zhu,

We wish to refer you to our order No.O123 for 500 cartons Niren Zhang craftworks, from which you will see that this order was placed on CFR basis.

As we now desire to have the consignment insured at your end, we shall be much pleased if you will kindly arrange to insure the goods on our behalf against All Risks at invoice value plus 10%, that is, USD3,000 as per the China Insurance Clauses of January 1, 1981.We shall of course refund the premium to you upon receipt of your debit note.

Looking forward to your early reply.

Yours faithfully,

Francis Steve

Vice President

11.3.2 Letter Two

(A Reply to the Above)

TIANJIN INTERNATIONAL IMP. & EXP. CO., LTD.

25 Zhujiang Street

TIANJIN, CHINA

TEL: …

E-Mail:tjiie_cl@tjiiecl.com

Fax: …

September 10, 2018

Mr.Francis Steve

Vice President

Thompson Consumption Group

5… Real Avenue

Sydney, Australia

Dear Mr. Steve,

Re: Your order No.O123 for 500 cartons Niren Zhang craftworks.

We have received your letter of September 4, asking us to effect insurance on the shipment for your account.

We are pleased to inform you that we have covered the shipment with the People's Insurance Company of China against All Risks for USD 1,350.00.The policy is being prepared accordingly and will be forwarded to you by next Monday together with our debit note for the premium.

Yours faithfully,

Zhu Gui

Manager

11.3.3 Letter Three

(Request for Excessive Insurance)

LEGEND.CO., LTD

…Street

ROTTERDAM , HOLLAND

TEL: …

E-Mail:legend_cl@legendcl.com

Fax: …

May 29, 2018

Hua Sheng Import & Export Corp.

3… Liberation Street

Shanghai, China

Dear Sirs,

We wish to refer you to our order No. 0401 for 1,000 cases clothes, from which you will see that this order was placed on CIF basis. Please note that we do not cover Strikes Risk, so please delete the word "Strikes Risk" in the insurance clause in the credit.

We know you only cover All Risks in general situation. In fact we would like to add War Risk because of the complicated situation in the Middle East. Can you get this for us? We shall of course bear the premium for this sort of special coverage.

We sincerely hope we have now made our position clear and our request will meet with your approval.

Yours faithfully,

Hua Sheng

Manager

11.3.4 Letter Four

(Application for Insurance)

NEW CONCEPT CO., LTD.

P.O.BOX 599

MACAO

TEL: …

E-Mail:tjiie_cl@tjiiecl.com

Fax: …

April 10, 2018

People's Insurance Company of China

28 Qinghuaxi Street

Haidian Zone, Beijing

China

Gentlemen,

We have known that your company is the largest insurance company in China with branches and sub-branches throughout the country and with survey and claim settling agents in major ports of the world. We wish to insure with your company a shipment of children bicycles against All Risks at invoice value plus 10%.

The details are as follows:

From Tianjin to Australia, 2,000 cases bicycles, by s/s China Hero, due to leave Tianjin on April 15.

The invoiced value of the consignment including freight and commission is USD 75,500.

Your early reply will be appreciated.

Yours faithfully,

Well Smith

Vice Manager

11.3.5　Letter Five

(The Requirement to Increase the Rate of Insurance)

LEGEND CO., LTD.
…Street
ROTTERDAM , HOLLAND
TEL: …
E-Mail:legend_cl@legendcl.com
Fax: …

June 8, 2018

Lucky Textile Trade Co., Ltd.
123 Xinhua Street
Guangzhou, China

Dear Sirs,

　　We refer to our purchase confirmation No.100 for 500 pieces of Lucky Blanket. We are notifying that we have opened a Confirmed Irrevocable Letter of Credit No.200 through Citi Bank, totaling USD 3,500, the L/C shall remain in force till 30 June.

　　Please see to it that articles mentioned above would be shipped before the end of June and the goods should be covered insurance for 130% of the invoice value against All Risks. We know that in accordance with your usual practice, you cover the goods only for 10% above the invoice value. Therefore the extra premium will be for our account.

　　Please arrange insurance as our requirements and we await your advice of shipment.

Yours faithfully,
David Beckham
President

11.4　Words and Phrases

1. **acknowledge**　*v.*　to report the receipt of　告知已收到
2. **assure**　*v.*　to make certain; ensure　向……保证；使……确信
3. **arrange**　*v.*　dispose something　安排；排列；协商
4. **breakage**　*n.*　loss or damage as a result of breaking　破碎
5. **cover**　*v.*　transact insurance　保险；投保

6. **claim**   *n.*   a demand for payment in accordance with an insurance policy or other formal arrangement   索赔

7. **insure**   *v.*   to cover with insurance   投保；保险

8. **insurance**   *n.*   an agreement by contract to pay money in case of a misfortune such as damage, loss or accident   保险

9. **insurer**   *n.*   one that insures, especially an insurance underwriter   保险人

10. **insured**   *n.*   the party who stands to benefit from an insurance policy   投保人；被保险人

11. **premium**   *n.*   a payment made to buy insurance   保险金

12. **invoice value**   the value of invoice   发票价值

13. **on one's behalf**   to represent someone   代表某人或某方

14. **assure sb. of sth.**   to make someone feel certain of having something   向某人保证某事

15. **take sth. up with sb.**   to talk something with someone   向某人谈及某事

11.5   Notes

1. **As we now desire to have the consignment insured at your end...**   因我方欲使货物在贵方投保……

2. **this order was placed on CFR basis**   我们的订单是按成本加运费订购的

3. **effect insurance on the shipment for your account**   对货物代办保险

    effect   进行；实现；办理

    effect shipment   装货　　　　　**effect insurance**   办理保险

4. **to bear the additional cost**   承担附加费用

5. **the scope of coverage**   承保范围

6. **book the shipping space**   订舱位

7. **excessive insurance = additional insurance**   附加险

8. **refund the premium to you**   将保险费退还给你

9. **draw on us at sight**   开即期汇票向我方收款

10. **for your account**   记在你方账下；你方付费

11. **Ocean Marine Cargo Clauses**   海洋运输货物保险条款

    Institute Cargo Clauses(ICC)   （伦敦保险协会）协会货物条款

12. **We know that in accordance with your usual practice, you cover the goods only for 10% above the invoice value.**   我们知道按你方惯例只按发票金额的110%投保。

11.6   Useful Expressions

1. We can arrange insurance on your behalf.
我方可以为你方代办保险。

2. We have covered the goods against All Risks and TPND.

我们已为货物投保了一切险和偷窃、提货不着险。

3. Since the premium varies with the extent of insurance, extra premium is for the buyer's account, should additional risks be covered.

因为保险费随保险范围的不同而不同，如果买方要求投保附加险，额外的保险费由买方负担。

4. We shall refund to you the premium upon receiving your debit note or you may draw on us at sight for the amount required.

我们收到你方借项清单后返还保险费，或者你方按所付金额向我方开出即期汇票。

5. Insurance is to be effected by the sellers for 110% of the invoice value against All Risks and War Risk as per the relevant Ocean Marine Cargo Clause of the People's Insurance Company of China, dated January 1,1981.

由卖方根据中国人民保险公司 1981 年 1 月 1 日颁布的《海洋运输货物保险条款》按发票金额的 110%投保一切险和战争险。

6. Please see to it that the above-mentioned goods should be shipped before 15 May and the goods should be covered for 150% of invoice value against All Risks. We know that according to your usual practice, you insure the goods only for 10% above the invoice value, therefore the extra premium will be for our account.

请注意上述货物必须确保于 5 月 15 日前装船并按发票金额的 150%投保一切险。我方知道按照你方一般惯例只按发票价格加成 10%投保，因此额外保险费由我方负担。

7. Should stranding and sinking of the carrying vessel take place, then how would the insurance company handle this situation?

万一运输船搁浅沉没，保险公司将如何处理？

8. If the insured shall make any claim knowing the same to be false or fraudulent as regards amount or otherwise, this policy shall become void and all claim there under shall be forfeited.

若被保险人故意虚报保额或其他项目，则该保险单无效，且被保险人丧失索赔权。

11.7 Exercises

1. Choose the best answer.

(1) Will you please _____ to take out All Risks insurance for us on the following consignment?

    A. help   B. arrange   C. cover   D. insure

(2) Insurance is to be _____ by the buyer if a transaction is concluded on FOB or CFR basis.

    A. taken   B. covered   C. done   D. made

(3) We will refund the premium _____ you _____ receipt of your debit note.

    A. to, upon   B. with, upon   C. to, at   D. with, at

(4) We think your price is offered _____ high level.

    A. on the　　　　　　B. at a　　　　　　C. on a　　　　　　D. at the

(5) _____ Mr. Smith told me, he would import garments from China in the near future.

    A. According as　　　　　　　　　　B. According with

    C. According to　　　　　　　　　　D. In according with

(6) We rely on receiving your reply _____.

    A. in return　　　　B. by return　　　　C. on return　　　　D. with return

(7) Which of the following is a Principle Risk?_____

    A. TPND.　　　　B. Risk of Shortage.　　C. War Risk.　　D. All Risks.

(8) Please insure _____ Leakage Risk(Breakage Risk, Fresh Water Damage Risk).

    A. on　　　　　　B. at　　　　　　C. with　　　　　　D. against

(9) Any loss or damage noticed when the goods are delivered must be reported to the _____ at the time, otherwise he will not be liable for it.

    A. carrier　　　　B. shipper　　　　C. consignor　　　D. consignee

(10) We will _____ the premium to you _____ receipt of your debit note.

    A. refund, upon　　B. give, in　　　　C. send, at　　　D. mail, in

2. Translate the following sentences into English.

（1）我们是按 FOB 价达成交易的，所以应由你方投保。

（2）如果没有你们的明确指示，我们将按一般惯例投保平安险和战争险。

（3）我们应按发票金额的 110%投保水渍险。

（4）破碎险的保险费率为 5%，如果你方愿意投保破碎险，我们可以代为办理。

（5）我们附上一份检验证书和船运代理的声明，并希望上述索赔金额达 5000 美元的理赔不会存在困难。

（6）你们保险公司通常承保什么险别？

（7）保险索赔应尽早提交给保险公司或其代理人，以便保险公司或其代理人有足够的时间向相关过失方追偿。

（8）客户无具体要求时，我方通常投保水渍险和战争险。若贵方想投保平安险，请预先告知。

3. Translate the following sentences into Chinese.

(1) For the coverage of All Risks the insurance company shall be liable for total or partial loss on land or sea of the insured goods within the period covered by the insurance.

(2) We adopt the warehouse to warehouse clause which is commonly used in international insurance.

(3) As our order was placed on a CIF basis and you took out insurance, we should be grateful if you would take the matter up for us with the insurance company.

(4) We ask you to insure risks of Strikes, Riots & Civil Commotion on the consignment.

(5) When definite insurance cannot be covered on account of the ship's being unconfirmed. please insure against provisional insurance and change it to definite insurance at the time of ship's confirmation.

(6) Premium will be added to invoice amount together with freight charges.

(7) Since the premium varies with the extent of insurance, extra premium is for buyer's account, should additional risks be covered.

4. Write a letter according to the information given in the following situations, applying the writing principles discussed in this chapter.

> 我公司订购了 200 台电脑，合同号为 704。
>
> 我公司已通过伦敦中国银行开出保兑不可撤销信用证，编号为 188 号，金额为 3600 美元，有效期至 2018 年 10 月 11 号。
>
> 按发票金额 120%投保一切险，鉴于你方惯例只按 110%的发票金额投保，故额外保险费由我方承担。
>
> 我方等待贵方的装船通知。

Answers for Reference

Chapter 12　Agency

12.1　Introduction

It is known that international business relations are established not only by a direct way, namely the business negotiation between exporters and importers, but also by an indirect way, that is, agency. Agency is a usually international practice that an agent is appointed to act as a marketing behavior, such as selling or purchasing. An important reason for appointing a foreign agent is his/her knowledge of local conditions and of the market in which he/she will operate. He knows what goods are best suits to this area and what prices the market will bear.

When we choose a firm or a person to be our agent, we should make sure whether he has sufficient means to develop the trade and whether the firm or person has reliable connections in the area. Once the relationship is set up, an agreement of agency is needed to bind the principal and the agent to act in strict accordance with the provisions of the agreement.

The agent is obliged to sell the goods actively and render market report. He will get a commission from the principal according to the turnover or a percentage of the price of the goods in return, maybe a fee.

There are mainly two types of agents: general agent and sole agent (exclusive agent). The general agent has a full authority from the principal and can not only sign contract directly with the customer on his principal's behalf but also deal with other commercial activities in a certain region. However, the sole agent can only enjoy the full privilege of exclusive sales for some kinds of goods in certain district within a certain period.

12.2　Writing Guide

When you are ready to act as an agent for a foreign firm, you need to ask for sole agent. The essential elements are as follows.

(1) Express your wishes to represent as their sole agent.

(2) Explain why you think an agent is needed.

(3) List your advantages serving as an agent.

(4) What terms you can accept.

If you are a company who is seeking for sole agent to expand your business, the letter should be written like this:

(1) The reason why you want to appoint agent.

(2) The reason why you choose this company to represent for you.

(3) The terms of agency you can provide.

12.3　Letters for Example

12.3.1　Letter One

(Asking for Sole Agency)

Dear Sirs,

We understand that you have no agent in China and we would like to offer services.

For the past six years we have been selling various durable goods to wholesalers and large retailers in all parts of China, and have built up a considerable number of well-established connections showing excellent business results.

Until recently we were not in the position to look for additional lines, as we were concentrating our efforts on sales of other lines. However, we have now enough ability to expand our sales, and if you agree to grant us a sole agency we will devote full attention to promote your products on China market.

If you are interested in our proposal, we should be pleased to provide our bank and trade reference.

Yours faithfully,

12.3.2　Letter Two

(Appointing Agency)

Dear Sirs,

We have duly received your letter of October 20, 2018. Thank you for your proposal of acting as our agent. After a careful study of your business reputation and your financial standing, we are glad to inform you that we have decided to entrust you with the sole agency for our textiles in the territory of China.

The appointment will be for a trial period of one year in the first instance. We shall pay you a commission of 7% on the net value of all sales against orders received through you.

If you will confirm these terms, we will arrange for a formal agreement to be drawn.

We shall do all in our power to assist you in establishing a mutually beneficial trade.

Yours faithfully,

12.3.3 Letter Three

(Seeking for Agency)

Dear Sirs,

We are one of the world's leading manufactures of textile products in England and have exported our products to several countries. Recently after doing a market research we find that there are good prospects of a very profitable market in your country.

Due to your good connections with the local customers in China, we are confident that you are in a good position to expand our business in your market. Our cooperation would mainly depend upon your terms and conditions. As our representative Mr. Zhang Hua will visit China next week, we think it would be better to discuss this issue with him.

Please let us know if you would accept the offer and your terms and conditions. We hope our cooperation will be successful.

Yours faithfully,

12.3.4 Letter Four

Confirmation of Agency Terms

Dear Sirs,

Thank you for your letter of April 14, 2018 offering to appoint us as your sale agent in the Unite State of America. Before drafting the sole agent agreement to be signed by both sides, we would like to confirm the following major points.

(1) That we act as your sole agent for a trial period of twelve months, starting from 1 December.

(2) That you pay us a commission of 5% on our sales of your products.

(3) That we do not commit to selling the competing products of other manufactures.

(4) That we render monthly statements of sales and quarterly summaries of sales activity.

(5) That we maintain a full range of your products in our showrooms.

We look forward to your confirmation to the above points and to be your sole agent.

Yours faithfully.

12.4 Words and Phrases

1. **establish** *v.* to start having a relationship with someone or to start discussions with them

建立（业务关系）

2. **commission**　*n.*　a (system of) payment to someone who sells goods which is directly related to the amount of goods　佣金

3. **on one's behalf**　为……的利益；代表

e.g.　His final act would be a single transcendent gesture on their behalf.　最后这一行动将是为他们着想而做出的一项不平凡的姿态。

4. **as follows**　*adv.*　如下所述

5. **reputation**　*n.*　prestige　名誉；名声

6. **proposal**　*n.*　something proposed (such as a plan or assumption)　提议；建议

7. **entrust**　*v.*　to give as a trust to (someone)　委托；托付

常用用法有：entrust sb. with sth.　委托某人做某事　entrust sth. to sb.　把某事委托某人

8. **profitable**　*adj.*　resulting in or likely to result in a profit or an advantage　有利可图的

9. **depend upon**　依赖；取决于

e.g.　We have to depend upon his good sense to save us all.　我们还要靠他的良知来搭救我们大家。

10. **representative**　*n.*　one that serves as a delegate or an agent for another　代表

11. **commit**　*v.*　perform an act, usually with a negative connotation　承诺；犯罪；做错事；使……承担义务

commit oneself to　致力于

12. **render**　*vt.*　to submit or present　呈递；提交

12.5　Notes

1. **sole or exclusive agent**　独家代理

2. **durable goods**　耐用品

3. **have built up a considerable number of well-established connections showing excellent business results.**　已经建立数量可观的良好销售网并显示了出色的业务业绩。

4. **Until recently we were not in the position to look for additional lines, as we were concentrating our efforts on sales of other lines.**　眼下我们没有能力寻找更多的产品，因为我们正集中精力销售其他产品。

5. **...if you agree to grant us a sole agency we will devote full attention to promote your products on China market.**　如蒙贵公司同意我们成为您的独家代理，本公司会竭尽全力为贵公司产品在中国建立起市场。

6. **commission**　*n.*　佣金

a commission of 5%/5% commission　5%的佣金

two items of commission　两笔佣金

Draw(receive) a commission of 5% on each sale　在每笔生意中抽取（收取）5%的佣金

The above price includes your 2% commission　以上所开价格包括你方 2%的佣金

7. **That we commit not to sell the competing products of other manufacturers.**　我们保证不销售其他厂商的同类竞争产品。

8. **monthly statements of sales**　月销售报告

12.6　Useful Expressions

1. After three years of mutual cooperation in this business, we should like to act as your agent in our city in order to most effectively market your products.

经过三年在该贸易领域的相互合作，为了更有效地推广贵方产品，我们愿意成为贵方在我们所在城市的代理。

2. We should be glad if you would consider our application to act as agent for the sale of your plastic slippers.

如果你方能够考虑我方关于成为你方塑料拖鞋销售代理的申请，我们将非常高兴。

3. Your proposal to be our sole agent is under serious consideration. In reply, we would like to know your detailed plan for handling our products, your sales channels, prospective sales turnover and your commercial and financial references so that we can decide on your proposal.

我们正在认真考虑你方提出成为我方独家代理的申请。在做出决定之前，我们希望了解你方有关代理我方产品的具体计划、你们的销售渠道、预计的销售额以及商界和金融界证明人的名单。

4. Thank you for your proposal of acting as our agent. In view of your past efforts in pushing the sale of our products, we have decided to accept your proposal and appoint you as sole agent.

感谢你方提议成为我方代理，考虑到你方过去推销我方产品的努力，现决定接受你方提议，委派你方为独家代理。

5. After careful consideration, we have decided to entrust you with the sole agency for Textiles in the territory of China.

经过仔细考虑，决定委托你方为我们纺织品在中国地区的独家代理。

6. We think that it would be premature to commit ourselves at this stage when the record of transaction shows only a moderate volume of business.

我们认为现在做出承诺为时过早，因为交易的记录显示目前的交易额尚不太可观。

7. Referring to the question of sole agency, we are not yet prepared to take the matter into consideration for the time being. We shall revert to this subject as soon as the business between us has developed to our mutual satisfaction.

关于独家代理问题，目前我们还不准备考虑此事。但当彼此业务发展至双方都感到满意时，我们可以再谈此事。

12.7   Exercises

1. Fill in the blanks with the words given below.

consider	effective	sufficient	entitle	act
represent	well-trained	extent	appoint	effort

(1) If you are not already represented here, we should be interested in _____ as your sole agent.

(2) We would appreciate it if you could _____ our proposal of sole agent.

(3) As we have learned that you are anxious to _____ your activity in our market and are not represented at present.

(4) _____ you, we have the confidence of outdistancing out competitors.

(5) We have _____ canvassing ability to be your sole agent.

(6) We can be a good agent because we have a group of _____ salesmen.

(7) If you give us the agency we should spare no _____ to further your interests.

(8) We trust that our experience in international trade and marketing will _____ us to your confidence.

(9) If you can push the sales of our products successfully for the next six months, we may _____ you as our agent.

(10) To be our agent, you are requested to push the sales of our products _____.

2. Translate the following sentences into Chinese.

(1) We firmly believe that an agency for marketing your products in Poland would be of considerable benefits to both of us.

(2) The agency agreement has been drawn up for the duration for one year, automatically renewable on expiration for similar period unless written notice is given to the contrary.

(3) We are confident that a close cooperation between us will lead to more brisk sales of our products on your market.

(4) If your work turns out to be satisfactory, the agreement can be renewed on expiry. We shall consider a longer period at that time.

(5) We shall study carefully your suggestion, but we should like to know first your sales volume and your plan for promoting our products.

(6) To be our sole agent, you could not sell similar products from other manufactures without our prior approval.

(7) For your reference, we would propose a sole agency agreement for a duration of three years with annual turnover of 50,000, 60,000 and 70,000 pieces for the first, second and third year

respectively.

3. Translate the following letter into Chinese.

Dear Sirs,

We are grateful to your inquiry regarding sole agent for the sale of our Man-made Leather Bags in Poland.

After serious consideration, we decided not to commit ourselves at this stage, when the record of transaction shows only a moderate volume of business.

Please do not misinterpret our above remarks. They do not imply any dissatisfaction. We are quite satisfied with the mount of business you have done with us. However, we are of the opinion that a bigger turnover must be reached to justify establishing an agency. We think it advisable to postpone this matter until your future sales warrant such a step.

We hope you will appreciate our position and continue giving us your cooperation.

Yours faithfully,

Answers for Reference

Chapter 13   Complaints and Claims

13.1   Introduction

In the international business, complaints do not happen in every transaction but often occur. Because once the contract is established, both the buyer and seller are obliged to observe all the terms and clauses in the contract. If one party violates or fails to carry out the contract, the other party is entitled to claim for any loss or damage. The reasons why buyers make complaints or raise claims including: inferior quality, wrong dispatch, short weight, damaged goods, improper packing, non-delivery, etc. However, the sellers may also lodge claims against buyers for non-establishment of L/C or breach of contacts.

Sometimes the party who suffered the loss may just make a complaint instead of lodging a claim if the loss or damage is not serious in order to keep their friendly relationship. It can also save time and cost. The purpose of a complaint is not only to express dissatisfaction but also to call the faulty party's attention to such things that should never happen again.

If the complaint can't be resolved satisfactorily, one can further lodge a claim. While a claim is more formal, it should be attached with the evidence presented through a careful checkup.

However, both the complaint letter and the claim letter are important to the company. In order to protect a company's reputation and image, equal attention must be given to both claim and complaint. It is favorable for the companies' relations if the complaints or claims are solved immediately and satisfactorily.

The purpose of writing a letter of complaint or claim is to solve the problems or get reasonable compensation instead of accusing the others. Accusing your reader is useless. It is more effective to focus on the problem which needs to be addressed. So the complaint or claim letter should be written in a restrained and tactful way.

13.2   Writing Guide

The purpose of writing a letter of complaint or claim is to solve the problem quickly and efficiently. So the letter should be written promptly, specifically and politely.

Usually a complaint or claim letter adopts the following steps.

(1) Expressing your regret, giving specific information including the order number, the date of delivery, the name of the ship and any other information about goods.

(2) Giving the detailed explanation clearly and impersonally, describing the loss, damage or inconvenience you suffered in a restrained and tactful way, asking for compensation.

(3) Giving you suggestion or requirement directly, hoping for an early reply.

When you reply to a complaint or claim, the letter also should be factual, courteous and fair. It should include the following elements.

(1) Expressing great regret about the matter and showing you will investigate the matter at once.

(2) After going into the matter, explain the reasons clearly. If your company should be responsible for the damage or loss, admit the mistake and indicate what you will do to settle the matter.

(3) If the responsibility is not yours, then explain clearly and give enough evidences to support you.

(4) Hoping the other party will be satisfied with the arrangement

13.3   Letters for Example

13.3.1   Letter One

(Complaint for Inferior Quality)

Dear Sirs,

Re : Our Order No. 123

We have received the 100 pieces of Cotton Prints under our Order No.123 you shipped per s.s. "Peace". Upon unpacking the bales, however, we were surprised to find that the goods were inferior to the sample originally submitted by you. The material seems to be roughly made and is inclined to be out of shape, the shade being much lighter.

We have sent you a sample of this article by separate mail so you can compare it with your original sample.

The inferior quality of the goods causes us considerable difficulty and it is hard for us to dispose of it. We can't accept and sell the goods so unsuited. So for the sake of our long and friendly cooperation ,we hope you can look into the matter at once and arrange for the dispatch of the goods we ordered immediately.

Look forward to your early reply.

Yours faithfully,

13.3.2　Letter Two

(Complaint for Wrong Goods)

Dear Sirs,

Re: Our Order No.123

Thank you for your prompt fulfillment of our order No.123. Everything appears to be correct and in good condition except Case No.2.

When examining the goods, we found that Case No.2 contained the wrong articles. We presume that there must have been some mistakes in making up the order.

Your wrong delivery has caused us much trouble as we are in urgent need of the goods to go ahead with our production.

Please arrange for the dispatch of replacement at once and meanwhile let us know what you wish us to do with Case No.2.

Yours faithfully,

13.3.3　Letter Three

(Complaint for Non-delivery)

Dear Sirs,

We placed an order for 500 dozens of silk blouses on March 10 and the order was scheduled for delivery on April 15. But to our surprise, we have not yet received the goods or any advice from you when we can expect delivery. As you have been informed in our previous letter that our customer is in urgent need of the goods, we hereby ask you to dispatch the silk blouse without any possible delay.

We must point out to you that this delay is very seriously inconvenient for us, and we ask you to give the reason of the non-execution of our order. If you are not in the position to ship the goods within a week, we shall have no alternative but to cancel the contract. We hope you will look into the matter at once and let us know what you propose to do.

Yours faithfully,

13.3.4　Letter Four

(Claim for Damaged Goods)

Dear Sirs,

The enamelware under our Order No.123 shipped per s. s. "Great wall" arrived at Port Shanghai on March 25.

Thanks for your prompt delivery. But much to our regret, when we opened the cases, we found that 3 boxes were seriously damaged and the enamelware shattered into pieces.

We immediately invited qualified surveyors to the spot to look into the case, and their findings showed that this was due to poor packing. The wooden cases were not strong enough for long distance voyage. There were not enough shockproof pads inside the boxes.

To support our claims, we enclose a copy of Survey Report together with our Statement of Claim which amounts to RMB 20,000.

We shall be glad if you will look into the matter as one of urgency. Look forward to your early reply.

Yours faithfully,

13.3.5   Letter Five

(Claim for Short Weight)

Dear Sirs,

Re: our Order No.123 for 20 M/T Chemical Fertilizer

We have just received the Survey Report from Shanghai Commodity Inspection Bureau evidencing that the captioned goods unloaded here yesterday was short weight of 800 kg. As you know, we have been in urgent need of these items as we have only a few in stock.

A thorough examination showed that the short weight was due to the improper packing, for which the suppliers should be definitely responsible. According to the Survey Report, we hereby lodge a claim against you for RMB 16,000 in all.

We are enclosing a copy of the Survey Report and look forward to settlement at an early date.

Yours faithfully,

13.4   Words and Phrases

1. **complaint**   *n.*   statement about things being dissatisfactory   抗议；申诉
常用搭配：make/lodge/lay a complaint against

2. **claim**   *n.*   a demand for compensation   索赔
   claim on the goods   对该货物提出索赔
   claim for inferior quality   由于品质低劣而索赔
   claim for US ＄10,000   提出金额为 1 万美元的索赔
   claim against a person   向某人提出索赔

3. **transaction**   *n.*   the act of transacting within or between groups (as carrying on commercial activities)   交易；办理；处理；事务

4. **violate**   *v.*   break an oath, a treaty, etc. act contrary to what one's conscience tells one to

do, etc. 违反；违背；侵犯；亵渎

5. **reasonable** *adj.* showing fairness and sense 通情达理的；合理的；适度的；公道的

6. **reputation** *n.* what is generally said or believed about the abilities, qualities, etc. of sb./sth. 名气；名声；名誉

7. **be inclined to** *conj.* be willing to accept. 倾向于；易于

8. **dispose** *v.* to settle or decide a matter 处理；处置；部署

9. **prompt** *adj.* (of an action) done quickly, at once, or at the right time (of a person) arriving at the right time 立刻的；迅速的；及时的；准时到达的

10. **presume** *vt.* to take for granted as being true in the absence of proof to the contrary 假定；假设；认为

11. **in need of** *vt.* want, require, deserve 需要

12. **schedule** *v.* plan for an activity or event; make a schedule; plan the time and place for events 排定；将……列表；为……作目录

13.5 Notes

1. **focus on** 集中于

e.g. We must focus our attention on efficiency.
  我们必须把注意力集中在效率上。

2. **Upon unpacking the bales, however, we were surprised to find that the goods were inferior to the sample originally submitted by you.** 然而，一打开箱子，我们很吃惊地发现货物的质量低于之前您发来的样品的质量。

3. **compare with** equals to compare to 与……相比

e.g. I'm afraid my English compares poorly with hers.
  恐怕我的英语同她相比要差得多。

4. **for the sake of** 为了……的利益

  for the sake of someone 为了某人的利益

e.g. We make concessions for the sake of peace.
  为了和平我们做出了让步。

5. **arrange for the dispatch** 安排发货

6. **But to our surprise, we have not yet received the goods or any advice from you suggesting/about when we can expect delivery.** 令我们奇怪的是，我们至今仍未收到货物，也没有从你处得到任何关于发货时间的通知。

7. **have no alternative** 别无选择

e.g. I have no alternative but to go with you.
  我除了跟你走以外别无选择。

8. **If you are not in the position to ship the goods within a week, we shall have no**

alternative but to cancel the contract. 如果你们不能在一周内装船，我们除了取消合同外别无选择。

9. **much to our regret** 令我们遗憾的是

e.g. Much to my regret, I have to leave now.
　　很遗憾，我得走了。

10. **Survey Report** 检验报告

Survey Report on Quality 品质鉴定证明书

Survey Report on Weight 重量鉴定证明书

Survey Report on Examination of Damage or Shortage 检验残损证明书

11. **Shanghai Commodity Inspection Bureau** 上海商品检验检疫局

13.6　Useful Expressions

1. You have confirmed our order, but to our surprise, we have not yet received the goods or any advice from you about when we may expect delivery.

你方已确认我方的订单，但奇怪的是我方至今尚未到货也未收到何时可以交货的信息。

2. We are still without your Advice of Dispatch of the cameras, while we are receiving urgent request from customers and you will understand that this delay places us in an awkward position.

我方仍未收到你方照相机的装运通知，但连续接到我方客户的催促，望你方明白，这次延误使我方处于困境。

3. On comparing the goods received with the samples, we were surprised to find that the color was not the same.

将收到的货物与样品比较后，我们惊讶地发现颜色不同。

4. The quality of your shipment for our Order No.123 has been found not in conformity with the agreed specification. We must therefore lodge a claim against you for the amount of RMB 30,000. The CCIB survey report is forwarded herewith and your early settlement is requested.

你方所发来我方第 123 号订单项下货物的质量与协议的规格不符。在此特向你方提出金额为三万元人民币的索赔。随附中国商品检验检疫局的检验报告，请早日解决该问题。

5. The goods delivered are not up to the standard of samples. The pattern is uneven in places and the coloring various.

所交货物未达到样品的质量标准，多处花样不匀，颜色各异。

6. We regret to point out that a shortage in weight of 210 lbs was noticed when the goods arrived.

遗憾地告知，货物到达时短重 210 磅。

7. The wrong pieces may be returned per next available steamer for our account, but it is preferable if you can sell them out at our price in your market.

错发的货物可由下一班货轮发回我处，费用由我方负担，但最好能将该货物在你方市场按我方价格抛售。

8. As the damage is apparently due to rough handling in transit, it is only appropriate for you to file your claim with the insurance company concerned.

显而易见，损坏是由于粗暴装卸所致，你应向相关保险公司索赔。

9. We have taken delivery of our order No.324. But much to our regret, only 5,420 cases were found against the 6,500 cases in the packing list.

我们已经提取了我方第 324 号订单下的货物。但遗憾的是，我们只收到 5420 箱货物，而不是装箱单中所列的 6500 箱。

10. This is the maximum concession we can make. Should you not agree to accept our proposal, we would like to submit the case to arbitration.

这是我方所能做出的最大让步。如你方不接受我们的建议，我方要将此事交予仲裁机构。

11. Your claim and the Survey Report are now having our careful consideration. We apologize to you for this unfortunate matter and assure you that your claim will be treated with promptness.

我们正在认真地考虑你方的索赔和检验报告。对这一不幸事件我们向贵方表示歉意并保证及时处理你方的索赔。

12. The goods were in perfect condition on leaving our warehouse and the damage has evidently occurred in transit.

该货从公司仓库运出时完好无损，所出现的损伤显然是在运输途中造成的。

13. Please dispatch at once a replacement of this item exactly ordered by us.

请立刻补发与我方所订货物一致的替代品。

13.7　Exercises

1. Fill in the blanks with prepositions.

(1) The goods we ordered _____ February 12, 2008 have arrived _____ a damaged condition.

(2) Our customers complain that the goods are much inferior _____ quality to our samples.

(3) We are now lodging a claim _____ you _____ the short weight of fertilizer _____ our Order No.123.

(4) Our investigation shows that damage was caused _____ improper packing, so we have to refer the matter _____ you.

(5) The quality of your shipment for our order is not _____ conformity _____ the agreed specifications, we must therefore lodge a claim against you for the mount of RMB 30,000.

(6) We would like to know what you want us to do _____ the goods. Shall we return them to you or hold them _____ your disposal?

(7) As soon as the report is _____ our hands, we shall give the matter our best attention _____ a view to settling it at an early date.

(8) As the contracted time of delivery is rapidly falling due, it is imperative that we hear from you ＿＿＿＿ any further delay.

(9) The 500 computers we ordered arrived today. ＿＿＿＿ opening the containers we found that the goods were short ＿＿＿＿ 30 sets.

(10) We have to ask ＿＿＿＿ a compensation ＿＿＿＿ cover the loss incurred as a result of inferior quality of the goods concerned.

2. Translate the following sentences into Chinese.

(1) We regret to inform you that the goods received are not in accordance with your samples.

(2) We regret to have to complain about the late delivery of the goods ordered on May 12 because, as you know, punctual shipment is of vital importance to us.

(3) With the regards to the loss in weight, we are enclosing a surveyor's report in order to prove to you that the loss could only have occurred in transit.

(4) We had the material inspected immediately when the goods arrived, and a shortage of 50 M/T was found.

(5) This consignment is not up to the standard stipulated in the contract. We are now lodging a claim against you.

(6) Since we have very good relations with you, we are willing to accept the shipment if you will allow a 20% reduction in price.

(7) Our investigation shows that the breakage of the captioned goods is attributed to the inferior quality of the containers which do not come up to the standard for transit.

3. Write a letter to your customer including the following information.

（1）收到对方 5 月 24 日对于受损货物的申诉信并表示遗憾。

（2）表明货物离开时状态良好并出具清洁提单为证。推测受损货物可能是由于运输途中不当装卸所致。

（3）建议对方向船运公司索赔。

（4）表示愿意协助对方处理此事。

Answers for Reference

Chapter 14   Sales Promotion

14.1   Introduction

In foreign trade, it is truly important to establish new business relations and negotiate with customers, and sales promotion is also important to company. It plays a key role in developing trade. To some extent, sales letters are a form of advertising because they aim to sell particular kinds of goods or services to selected types of customers.

Sales letters are usually written by companies to their potential buyers, former customers and existing ones. The contents of sales letters are different according to the purposes, so it can be divided into three types: sales letter, reviver and follow-up letter. Generally sales letters are to introduce new products or promote ones to customers, informing them the new benefits or discount they can receive recently. However, the main purpose to write a sales letter is to get the attention and arouse the interest of the reader, convincing them that the goods or services you provide is beneficial to them.

An efficient sales letter should consist of four essential features: catching attention, arousing interest, creating desire and inducing action. Anyway, when we write a sales letter, we should observe the following rules which may be helpful.

(1) Catch the reader's interest in the opening paragraph, starting the letter with an attractive opening sentence.

(2) Keep the letter short, concise and luminous, or it may be deleted or thrown away.

(3) Introduce the features, advantages and benefits of the goods as accordant as possible.

(4) Emphasize the reader can benefit from the goods or services you provide.

(5) Give the letter an attractive look and make it as personal as possible.

14.2   Writing Guide

1. Writing Sales Letters

When you write to new customers in order to expand your business, you should adopt the following steps.

1) Arouse Interest

Remember to start your letter with an attractive opening sentence. If you fail to catch their eyes at the first sight, the letter may be neglected or deleted without reading.

2) Create Desire

Build interests by describing unique features and advantage of the products, such as being fashionable, romantic, convenient or healthy.

3) Carry Conviction

Increase desire by stressing the benefits that they can receive from purchasing at once.

4) Induce Action

Persuade your readers to act as you want after you have provided such appealing interests.

2. Writing a Reviver

Sometimes you have not received orders from your old customers for a long time. You need to write a reviver in order to rebuild relationship with them. The letter should contain the following elements:

(1) review the friendly relationship;

(2) recommend your new products;

(3) offer a generous discount;

(4) look forward to a new order.

3. A Follow-up Letter

When you have received an inquiry from a customer about your products or services, you have sent them a quotation. But you have not received any order. Now it's time to write a follow-up letter to ask about reasons and express the wish to conclude business with them. The following structure may be helpful:

(1) refer to the inquiry and the quotation;

(2) express regret and assume some possible reasons;

(3) emphasize new selling-point and advantage;

(4) expect to receive an order.

14.3   Letters for Example

14.3.1   Letter One

(A Sales Letter to Potential Customer)

Dear Sirs,

As you know, reports from all over the world confirm what we had known before we put the famous "Reliance" solid tyre on the market that it is the fulfilment of every car-owner's dream.

You are well aware of the weakness of the ordinary air-filled tyre-punctures, split outer covers under sudden stress and a tendency to skid on wet road surfaces, to mention a few of the motorist's chief complaints. Our "Reliance" tyre enables to offer your customers a tyre that is beyond criticism in those vital qualities of road-holding and reliability.

We could tell you a great deal more about these tyres, but prefer you to read the enclosed copies of reports from racing drivers, test drivers, motor dealers and manufactures.

You are already aware of our terms of dealing, but in order to encourage you to lay in a stock of the new solid "Reliance", we are prepared to allow you a special discount of 5% on any order received by the end of next month.

We are looking forward to hearing from you soon.

Yours sincerely,

14.3.2　Letter Two

(A Reviver Letter to An Old Customer)

Dear Mr. Smith,

We have not received your orders for the past six months. You placed regular orders with us from 2013 to 2018.

When we noticed that you didn't renew your contract at the beginning of this year, we thought it was a delay. But until six months have passed, we have not received your orders yet, we wonder maybe you have found another supplier.

We treat you as our valued customer and we hope we could build a friendly and solid relationship. If there was a problem between us, please let us know.

We are enclosing a copy of our latest catalogue for your reference. Considering we are good cooperative partners, we would like to give 5% discount on your next order.

Your favorable response is awaited.

Yours Sincerely,

14.3.3　Letter Three

(A Follow-up Letter)

Dear Sirs,

We wrote to you on October 15 in reply to your inquiry dated October 10 for air-conditioners. However, up to now, we haven't had the pleasure of hearing from you. Your silence leads us to think that there must be something that precludes you from making further inquiries.

Perhaps it is because that the catalogue we sent you shows only the standard type of air-conditioners, and it is probably you could not find the model you were looking for.

Now we enclose a copy of our latest catalogue for you reference. The catalogue includes a wide range of household electric appliances, including refrigerators, microwave ovens and so on. The qualities and prices compare favorably with those of other makers.

If you are interested in any one of the items in our catalogue, please don't hesitate to let us know. We will give you our lowest quotations upon receipt of your specific inquiries.

We look forward to concluding some business with you in the near future.

Yours faithfully,

Encl. a catalogue

14.3.4   Letter Four

(A Sales Letter)

Dear friends,

Are you tired of doing the same work everyday?

Are you complaining about lower working efficiency of your computer?

Are you trying to upgrade your computer system but reluctant to spend a lot of money?

Perhaps you will be interested in Upgrading Software. Its unique features are:

(1) compatible to your current software and database;

(2) monitor the sales of products;

(3) process various documents and forms quickly;

(4) easy operation.

The program can increase the efficiency and help you earn more money. Why wait? Come and buy right now since a special discount of 20% will only be offered for three days.

Don't delay! Those who order during this period will save about RMB 180.

You can contact us by calling our toll-free number 022-11223344

Or email us: newsoftware@126.com

Yours faithfully,

14.3.5   Letter Five

(Product Promotion)

Dear Mr. James,

Great interest was aroused at the recent Arts & Crafts product exhibition in Shanghai by the large carpet manufacture in China. Numerous inquiries and orders have also come for the beautiful hand-woven carpets.

The preferred carpets are as follows:

Appearance: elegant designs with different sizes catering for the customer's needs.

Prices: superb quality with prices much lower than those from other sources.

Comfort: carpets are made from wool and silk, so they are giving the feeling of natural warmth and comfort.

You will be interested to note that our annual production is 10,000 pieces. Recently we have received inquiries from Japan, Australia, and Africa. We are convinced that our carpets will be exported to more countries in the near future.

We are glad to enclose our illustrated catalogue, and will send you our best quotation as soon as we hear from you.

Yours sincerely,

14.4 Words and Phrases

1. **induce** *vt.* cause to act in a specified manner; cause to occur rapidly 诱导；引起；引诱；感应

e.g. People are always induced by advertisements to buy things they don't really need.
人们总是受广告的诱惑，买一些自己并不真正需要的东西。

2. **reliability** *n.* the quality of being dependable or reliable 可靠性

e.g. Quality and reliability became Toyota's selling point.
质量和可靠性已经成为日本丰田汽车的卖点。

3. **preclude** *vt.* keep from happening or arising; make impossible 排除；妨碍；阻止

4. **catalogue** *n.* a list, usually in the form of a book, esp. 目录（也可写作 catalog）

latest catalogue 最新目录

catalogue of material 材料目录

5. **brand** *n.* a specific line of manufactured goods, identified by the manufacturer's name or the registered trademark 样式；品牌

6. **compatible** *adj.* capable of existing or performing in harmonious, agreeable, or congenial combination with another or others 兼容的；能共处的；可并立的

7. **monitor** *v.* to keep close watch over; supervise 监控；监视

8 .**elegant** *adj.* displaying effortless beauty and simplicity in movement or execution 高雅的；优雅的；讲究的；

9. **superb** *adj.* surpassingly good 极好的；华丽的；宏伟的；

10. **enclose** *vt.* enclose or enfold completely with or as if with a covering 围绕；装入；放入封套

14.5   Notes

1. **to some extent**　在某种程度上

e.g.　To some extent, I can understand their attitude.
　　　在某种程度上，我能理解他的态度。

2. **consist of**　由……组成

e.g.　All electronic computers consist of five units although they are of different kinds.
　　　电子计算机虽然种类不同，但它们都是由五个部件组成的。

3. **selling-point**　卖点；产品特色

4. **When we noticed that you didn't renew your contract at the beginning of this year, we thought it was a delay.**　年初的时候当我们注意到你们没有续订合同的时候，我们以为仅仅是耽搁了。

5. **We treat you as our valued customer and we hope we could build a friendly and solid relationship.**　我们把您当成最重要的客户，我们希望能够和您保持友好长久的合作关系。

6. **We are enclosing a copy of our latest catalogue for your reference.**　随函附寄我公司最新的产品目录供贵方参考。

7. **up to now**　到目前为止

8. **Your silence leads us to think that there must be something that precludes you from making further inquiries.**　您的沉默使我们认为肯定有一些事情阻止了您进一步询价。

9. **household electric appliance**　家用电器

10. **The quality and prices compare favorably with those of other makes.**　我方产品在质量和价格方面都优于其他品牌。

11. **upon receipt of**　收到……后（即做什么）
　　类似用法：after receipt of, after we receive

e.g.　Upon receipt of your L/C, we will send the goods.
　　　收到你方信用证后我们立即发货。

12. **complaint about**　抱怨，相当于 complaint of

13. **Arts & Crafts product exhibition**　工艺品艺术展

14. **Numerous inquiries and orders have also come for the beautiful hand-woven carpets.** 大量的询盘和订单都是冲着漂亮的手织毛毯来的。

15. **cater for**　迎合；为……提供所需

16. **We are glad to enclose our illustrated catalogue, and will send you our best quotation as soon as we hear from you.**　我们很高兴附上我方带插图的目录一份，一旦收到你方的回信，我们将向贵方报出最优惠的价格。

14.6　Useful Expressions

1. In order to popularize these products, all the catalogue prices are subjected to a special discount of 20% during this month only.

为了推广这些产品，产品目录上所有价格在本月都享有 20% 的特殊折扣。

2. We are offering you goods of the very highest quality on unusually generous terms and would welcome your earliest orders.

我们将在特殊的优惠条件下为您提供优质的产品，欢迎您早日订购。

3. You will see that prices this season are slightly higher, but you will find that this is offset by marked improvements in almost every line.

您将看到本季价格有轻微上涨，但这一上涨可以被每一产品的显著改进所抵消。

4. We believe it will surely find a good/ready market in your country.

我们相信该产品在贵国市场一定会很畅销。

5. We are an exclusive exporter of parts and components of various types of motorcycles in this district and would take the liberty to send a quotation sheet covering our current range of this line for your reference. We hope you will find it interesting.

我们是本地区各种摩托车零部件的独家出口商，借此机会给您寄去现有该类产品的报价单供您参考。希望您对此感兴趣。

6. With a view to supporting your sales, we have specially prepared some samples of our new makes and are sending them to you, under separate cover, for your consideration.

为了支持你们的销售，我们特别准备了一些新产品的样本另外寄给你方供参考。

7. We take pleasure in enclosing the latest designs of our products, which are superior in quality and moderate in price and are sure to find a good market at your end.

我们荣幸地随函寄出我们产品的最新设计样式，这些新设计质量高、价格适中，肯定会在你方市场畅销。

8. Owing to its superior quality and reasonable price, our poplin has met with a warm reception and quick sale in most European countries. We think it is to your advantage to buy this item for sale in your market.

我们的府绸品质优良、价格公道，在大多数欧洲国家深受欢迎且十分畅销。我们认为订购我们的府绸在你方市场销售对你方有利。

9. Since the required articles are not available, we would like to recommend the under-mentioned products which can be supplied from stock for prompt shipment. This recommendation is made in the interest of both parties.

由于您所需的品种目前无货供应，我们想推荐下列可立即发货的库存产品。我们这一推荐是基于照顾双方利益做出的。

10. We believe that you will take advantage of this opportunity to offer your customer with first-class products.

我们确信您会把握此机会去向贵公司客户提供一流的产品。

11. To encourage you to place orders with us, we would allow for a 3% special discount for any order received at the end of September.

为了鼓励贵方向我方下订单，特对九月底之前的订单给予3%的优惠折扣。

14.7 Exercises

1. Translate the following phrases into English.

（1）价格公道　　　（2）质量上乘

（3）工艺精湛　　　（4）设计新颖

（5）式样优美　　　（6）款式典雅

（7）色泽和谐　　　（8）做工考究

2. Fill in the blanks with appropriate words.

(1) Our products are _____ _____ _____ _____ in your area.（享有很高声誉）

(2) We are _____ _____ _____ _____ sending you a copy of our latest catalogue.（冒昧地）

(3) We hope you will _____ full _____ _____ it.（充分利用）

(4) The goods we are offering you are _____ _____ _____ _____.（物有所值）

(5) We are _____ to _____ that you are one of the leading iron nail exports in U.S.A.（被告知）

(6) The above _____ goods lie within the scope of our business activities.（标题项下的）

(7) Should _____ items be _____ interest to you, please let us know.（任何一种）

(8) _____ _____ _____ your specific inquiry, we shall be glad to offer you without any delay.（一旦接到）

(9) We believe it will surely _____ _____ _____ _____ in your country.（畅销）

(10) In order to _____ you with our products, we are sending you several sample books by separate mail together with a price list.（使熟悉）

3. Translate the following letter into Chinese.

Dear Sirs,

Thank you for your letter of April 3 inquiring about our Ladies' leather shoes.

We have pleasure in enclosing three copies of our illustrated catalogue and price list of the shoes we produce. From these you will be able to see that we can offer you a very wide range of shoes and the styles are moderate and very popular. Under separate cover we are also sending you a sample pair of Ladies' shoes. You can see for your eyes from these that the quality is very high and the material used are of great grade.

We have been supplying high quality shoes to the West European and North America for many years and all our customers have shown every satisfaction with our products. We believe it will surely find a good market in your country.

We can allow you a 5% discount on an order worth RMB 5,000 or more.

We look forward to hearing from you in the near future.

Yours faithfully,

Answers for Reference

Chapter 15　Cross-border E-commerce

15.1　Introduction

Cross-border e-commerce can be defined in both broad and narrow sense.

In a narrow sense, cross-border e-commerce is almost equal to cross-border retailing, in which transaction parties in different countries reach agreements and settle accounts through the Internet and deliver or receive the goods via cross-border logistics.

In a broad sense, cross-border e-commerce equals electronic foreign trade. It's a kind of international business, in which the product display, negotiation and transaction are done via the Internet and goods are delivered through cross-border logistics.

With development of more than a decade, China cross-border e-commerce has experienced the periods of information publish, transaction platform and the current booming of B2C. It shows different characteristics in each stage. Since two years ago, as the public has paid increasing attention to cross-border e-commerce and participanted commit to the sector, there have been some new characteristics formed, including the following aspects.

1. Participants

Before 2012, micro and small businesses, individual merchants and online merchants were the participants. After 2012, the main participators in traditional trade like foreign trade companies, manufacturers and brand owners began to enter this sector and have gradually formed certain scale.

2. Industry Chain

Steps like marketing, customs clearance, commodity inspection, logistics and payment may affect the development of cross-border e-commerce. Considering that, cross-border e-commerce companies keep expanding their services and try to provide integrated service, the whole industry chain and the service chain of the industry are getting clearer and sounder.

3. Brand Operation

By taking China's advantage in manufacturing, selling cheap but good-quality goods and OEM were the main patterns of early cross-border e-commerce. In recent two years, many companies have started running their own brand. Especially some big companies begin to build their own platforms to introduce their brands to oversea market and increase their value.

Traditional foreign trade logistics is mainly carried out by sea, while in cross-border e-commerce transactions, logistics methods include E-Post, China Post Parcel, large commercial express (EMS, DHL, UPS), dedicated international logistics and overseas warehouse + overseas local logistics. This puts forward new requirements for the communication between buyers and sellers in transportation business.

The rise of overseas warehouses makes up for the problems of high cost and low timeliness of traditional logistics, and effectively supports the stronger development of cross-border e-commerce. Overseas warehouse means that cross-border e-commerce sellers set up warehouses in overseas regions to deliver goods to overseas destinations for storage in advance. After consumers purchase products on the online platform, the warehouses will respond quickly according to local sales orders and directly complete localized services such as commodity sorting, packaging, distribution and transportation. There are three main modes of overseas warehouse at present: seller's self-built warehouse, third-party cooperative overseas warehouse and e-commerce platform's self-built warehouse.

The model of self-built overseas warehouses by sellers refers to that enterprises with strong financial strength purchase and build overseas warehouses in overseas destinations by themselves according to their own business scope and needs, and solve the original outsourcing business such as declaration, customs clearance, transportation, warehousing and distribution, such as Global Tesco. Third-party overseas warehouse cooperation refers to the cooperation between cross-border e-commerce sellers and third-party overseas warehouse service enterprises to deliver goods to third-party enterprises' self-built warehouses by sea, land and air in advance for storage and distribution. The self-built model of e-commerce platforms relies on overseas warehouses established by major cross-border e-commerce platforms themselves to open the platform to third-party sellers, who store their goods in platform warehouses and integrate their inventories into the platform's global logistics network. At the same time, cross-border sellers bear the corresponding service, management and return logistics costs. The platform provides the seller users with warehousing, sorting, transportation, distribution and return services, such as Amazon's FBA and Wish's FBW.

15.2 Writing Guide

Cross-border e-commerce foreign trade English correspondence mainly uses E-mail, instant messaging software and SMS.

15.2.1   Writing Features of Business E-mail

1. Simple format

Writing business e-mails does not have to be rigidly adhere to the format of formal business letters. It is composed of the beginning, the body and the end. Generally, the e-mails always use block format. This kind of format is relatively simple, clear at a glance and easy to read.

2. Simple language

The purpose of business e-mails is to communicate with customers as soon as possible, and communicate effectively, so the language must be concise and to the point. Mainly have the following characteristics:

1) Acronyms used in high frequency

E.g: A. Pls send us ur sample asap, becoz this project is very IMP. (Extensive use of acronyms)

B. Please send us your sample as soon as possible, because this project is very important. (No acronyms used)

2) The use of terminology

E.g: Please advice the ETD(estimated time of departure), ETA(Estimated Time of Arrival)and fax the copy of B/L(Bill of Lading).

3) Colloquial expression bias

E.g: A. We appreciate your cooperation. (Similar brief conversation, casual)

B. Your cooperation will be appreciated. (More written, appeared to be very formal)

15.2.2   Writing Features of Instant Messaging Software and SMS

At present the foreign trade instant-messaging software commonly used on the Internet are Skype, Viber, Whatsapp, Facebook, Twitter, Wechat, QQ, Google Talk, TradeManager, Dunhuang Tong, etc. Internal mail is a service function designed to facilitate the exchange of business letters between members. It is similar to a mailbox. Instant messaging software and internal letters have the following writing characteristics.

(1) The language has immediacy, which is different from written language. Comparing with oral language, it is often written in short sentences and repetition, such as "all" "you see" "just" and other words. The style is simple and relaxed.

(2) It has the characteristics of Internet language. It often uses abbreviations, acronyms and sometimes emoticons. Since buyers and sellers come from different countries, grammar and spelling errors may also occur in the expressions.

15.2.3　Writing Skills

1. The Inverted Pyramid Form

The important content put in the front, with the narrative gradually expanded, the importance of the content is gradually weakening.

2. Have a Good Title

Subject is often ignored by writers in foreign trade. Good subject should be able to summarize the main content of the message, up to 35 letters in length, which can directly affect the customer's judgment on the importance of the message, thus increasing the chance of the message being read.

3. Prompt for important information

4. Complete information and pay attention to courtesy

Before you sending it, be sure to check it carefully. Don't send an email without attachment, and pay attention to courtesy.

15.3　Letters for Example

15.3.1　Letter One

Green Leaf Company

Shasan Road
Guangzhou, China
April 22, 2018

Capitol Cigar Ltd.
64 Delhi Road
Bombay, India

Dear Sir,

How are you?

This is Bob. I'm working for Green Leaf Company and we have our newest products to sell. They are very hot selling now.

Are you interested in Ipv box mod?

Ipv D2 box mod (newest)
Ipv4 100w temp control box mod (can be upgrated to 125 watt)
Ipv mini2 70w box mod

If you want to know more information, please contact me.

Yours faithfully,
Green Leaf Company
Manager

15.3.2　Letter Two

IPV Vamping Company

Futeng Road
Zhejiang, China
July 25, 2018

Box Mod Ltd.
33 Brown Street
Newcastle, UK

Dear Sir,

This is Bob. I'm working for IPV Vamping company.

My manager Eric told me that you want to order our new product IPV 5, so he let me contact you.

Our MOQ is 50 sets, the unit price is $36. Big order has better price. Can you please tell me how many sets do you want to order?

Yours faithfully,
IPV Vaping Company
Manager

15.3.3　Letter Three

Box Mod Ltd.

33 Brown Street
Newcastle, UK
July 26, 2018

IPV Vamping Company
Futeng Road
Zhejiang, China

Hi Bob,

    Thanks for the reply.
    Please give me best price on 100 units.
    Please give me price on IPV PURE X2N for 100 pcs.

Yours faithfully,
Box mod Ltd.
Manager

15.3.4　Letter Four

Capitol Cigar Ltd.

64 Delhi Road
Bombay, India
April 29, 2018

Green Leaf Company
Shasan Road
Guangzhou, China

Hi Bob,

    Payment sent via PayPal.

It was sent from one of our site's address: Payments@lighterusa.com.

Total was $6,335.00.

However I was not given a PI number so there were no notes.

Please let me know if you got payment. Thank you.

Yours faithfully,

Capitol Cigar Ltd.

Manager

15.3.5 Letter Five

Dear Madam,

Thank you very much for your full support!

I'm sorry the swimsuit is not suitable for you. Can that swimsuit be given as a gift? Or should we refund some of the payment as compensation? Just suggest that if you insist on returning or replacing the goods, we will follow up the next step.

We await your reply.

Yours faithfully,

Hosa Ltd.

Manager

15.3.6 Letter Six

Dear Valuable Customer,

Thanks for your order. The product has been arranged with care. You may trace it on the following website after two days:

http://www.17track.net/indexen.shtml

Kindly be noticed that international shipping would take longer time (7-21 business days for China Port, 3-7 for EMS). We sincerely hope it can arrive fast and you can be satisfied with our products and services.

As well, we would appreciate very much if you may leave us five-star appraisal and contact us first for any question, which is very important for us.

We highly treasure your business and look forward to serving you again in the near future.

Yours faithfully,

Mondo Co., Ltd.

Manager

15.4　Words and Phrases

1. **hot selling**　热销

2. **box mod**　电子烟

3. **temp control**　温度控制

4. **upgrate**　*vt.*　使升级；提升；改良品种

　　　　　　　n.　升级

5. **vape**　"vape"一词最早出现在 1980 年，可以用作动词，形容抽电子烟时吞云吐雾，也可以作为名词指"电子水烟"这一器具。

6. **vaping**　电子烟

7. **MOQ**　*abbr.*　最小订货量（Minimum Order Quantity）

8. **set**　*n.*　a group of things of the same kind that belong together and are so used　[数]集合；一套

9. **unit**　*n.*　an individual or group or structure or other entity regarded as a structural or functional constituent of a whole　单位；单元

10. **pcs**　即 pieces 的缩写，个、件的意思，是数量单位，不是计量单位，一般指复数。当销往国外的物品需要计算每件物品单位，要用到 pcs。

11. **PayPal**　*n.*　贝宝（全球最大的在线支付平台）

12. **PI**　形式发票（Proforma Invoice），卖方凭此预先让对方知晓如果双方将来以某数量成交之后，卖方要开给买方的商业发票的大致形式及内容。它是一种试算性质的货运清单。

13. **payment**　*n.*　a sum of money paid　付款；支付

14. **FBA**　Fulfillment by Amazon，即亚马逊物流服务，亚马逊将自身平台开放给第三方卖家，将其库存纳入亚马逊全球的物流网络，为其提供拣货、包装以及终端配送的服务，亚马逊收取服务费。

15. **door to door**　门到门，即由托运人负责装载的集装箱在其货仓或工厂仓库交承运人验收后，由承运人负责全程运输，直到送至收货人的货仓或工厂仓库交箱为止。这种全程连线运输，称为"门到门"运输，也叫"送货上门"。

16. **tracking number**　订单编号；快递追踪编号

17. **overseas warehouse**　海外仓

18. **in good condition**　货物情况良好

19. **logistics**　物流

15.5　Notes

1. 价格术语

FOB (Free On Board)　离岸价格；船上交货价格

CFR (Cost and Freight)　指在装运港船上交货，卖方需支付将货物运至指定目的地港所需的费用，但货物的风险是在装运港船上交货时转移。

CIF (Cost, Insurance and Freight)　到岸价

2. 法律术语

conciliation　*n.*　any of various forms of mediation whereby disputes may be settled short of Arbitration　调解；安抚

penalty　*n.*　a payment required for not fulfilling a contract　罚款；罚金

3. 银行术语

invoice　*n.*　an itemized statement of money owed for goods shipped or services rendered　发票；货物；发货单

reimbursement　*n.*　compensation paid (to someone) for damages or losses or money already spent　*etc.*　退还；偿还；赔偿

4. 运输术语

liner　*n.*　a large commercial ship (especially one that carries passengers on a regular schedule)　班轮；班机

charter　*vt.*　hold under a lease or rental agreement; of goods and services　包租

consigner　*n.*　the person who delivers over or commits merchandise　发货人；委托人；寄售人

5. 付款方式

L/C 信用证

D/A 承兑交单

D/P 付款交单

T/T 电汇

6. 缩略词

ASAP 尽快；**TBA** 等通知；**FYI** 供参考；**ETD** 估计离港期；**ETA** 估计到港期；**B/L** 提货单；**FCL** 整柜

7. 贸易行业中常用的词

DHL *abbr.* （Dalsey, Hillblom and Lynn，一家国际快递公司）敦豪速递公司

courier 特快专递

FedEx 联邦快递

ICC *abbr.* （International Chamber of Commerce） 国际商会

Airway Bill 空运单

send *vt.* cause to be directed or transmitted to another place 发送；寄

dispatch *vt.* send away towards a designated goal 发出

submit *v.* hand over formally 提供

forwarder *n.* 货运商

e-mail 电邮

enclose *v.* enclose or enfold completely with or as if with a covering 附上

invoice *n.* an itemized statement of money owed for goods shipped or services rendered 发票

advanced samples 出货前的样品

free sample 免费样品

approval *n.* the formal act of approving 核准

at your earliest convenience 尽早

by return 回复

favorable response 佳音

8. 其他缩写

BK: bank

TKS: thanks

15.6　Useful Expressions

1. 婉转、礼貌词

It would be a great help if you could make a prompt response for the damaged machine.
如果能对机器损坏的问题及时给予答复，我方将不胜感激。

Please inform us at your earliest convenience when you would like to come.
请尽快告知我们，你们何时能来。

2. 与国外客户进行业务往来时常用的省略句

(1) noted & thanks for your email. =I noted the content and thanks for your email.

(2) Hope you will effect the shipment ASAP. =We really hope you will effect the shipment as

soon as possible.

(3) Any further news about the pilot samples? = Please let me know if there are any further news about the pilot samples.

3. 使用套语

商务英文电子邮件常使用各种固定的套语，这为双方在遣词造句及内容的理解上节省了不少时间。

正文的起始句常用：

(1) Thank you for your inquiry of ×××× about …

(2) We are in receipt of your email of …

(3) Well received your inquiry with many thanks.

(4) We did have a great holiday. How about you? It should be also wonderful!

正文的结尾句常用：

(1) I am looking forward to …

(2) Awaiting your prompt response.

(3) Be sure we will have pleasing cooperation.

(4) Any doubt or other information needed, please feel free to let me know.

(5) Contact me now and you will get free sample for quality checking!

建立业务关系常用：

(1) We would like to introduce ourselves to you as…

(2) We are willing to enter into business relations with…

(3) We look forward to working with your company, and establishing a great and lucrative long-term business relationship between our two companies.

客户索要样品常用：

(1) The sample charges including the freight is…

(2) Sample is available. Could you let me know the potential quantity of your mass order before sending sample?

报价常用：

(1) We are glad to quote you our favorite price of…

(2) Please be advised that the following are our best quotation for…for your consideration.

(3) Please kindly check if the price is workable for you or not.

客户讲价时常用：

(1) The bitterness of poor quality remains long after the sweetness of low price is forgotten.

(2) There are a lot of suppliers who can do this item, but some are new in this field and some are with more or less 10 years experience. We are the latter one.

客户不回复，跟进时常用：

(1) For the ××× you were looking for, we have sent the relative information and price to you two days ago. What is your feedback to it? Do you want to start the sample making?

(2) For the ×××, are you still interested in the project? We are still waiting for your further news to move forward.

(3) It seems you have stopped the communication but I should tell you it is really a hot selling item recently. Are you still interested in moving forward?

(4) Have you got (or checked) the prices or not? May we know if we still have the opportunity to discuss about this project? Any comment by return will be much appreciated. It will be a big pleasure if we have opportunity to serve you in the near future.

向客户收款时常用：

(1) Could you please kindly arrange the sample cost by Alibaba trade assurance? If yes, I will draft the alibaba trade assurance to you and then send the samples to the address you provided.

(2) Would you please kindly arrange the payment by Paypal? Our Paypal account is…

(3) Looking forward to your payment information to release the sample.

(4) Which way do you want to pay for the sample charges: by trade assurance or PayPal?

发货后常用：

(1) It is pleased to inform you that the goods have been sent to you by FedEx under the tracking No.: ××××××. Please kindly track.

(2) Any comments upon receiving the sample, please feel free to let me know.

邮件中插有附件常用：

(1) Attached please find…

(2) Enclosed please find…

这些套语是在长期的国际贸易实践中形成的，频繁被广大商务人员使用。

15.7　Exercises

1. Translate the following English phrases into Chinese.

(1) exchange rate quotation

(2) discount quotation

(3) market quotation

(4) quote a price

(5) quote favorable terms

(6) fall within the scope of our business activities

(7) be in the market for

(8) illustrated catalogue

(9) Chinese makes

2. Translate the following abbreviations into Chinese.

(1) MOQ

(2) pcs

(3) PI

(4) ASAP

(5) TBA

(6) FYI

(7) ETD

(8) ETA

(9) B/L

(10) FCL

3. Translate the following sentences into English.

（1）市场变为对卖方有利。

（2）根据我们在澳大利亚销售园林工具的经验，我们相信这些产品很快将成为你方市场上的畅销品。

（3）我们十分感激你方的合作。

（4）希望你方能理解我方的处境。

（5）我方一位客户想要购买中国红茶。

（6）关于我方的资信情况，请向中国银行西安分行查询。

（7）我们有幸自荐，以期与你公司建立业务关系。

（8）我们专门从事中国棉织品的出口业务，愿与你方进行交易。

（9）我们有意在贵国寻求原油供应的机会。

（10）感谢您支付订单，我们将在 3 天内发运这些货物。

（11）我们查询了跟踪信息，发现您的包裹已经到达了英国的海关。

（12）跟踪信息显示您已经收到您的订货！请确保物品到达你处时状态良好。

（13）如果您对您所购买的物品和我们的服务感到满意，我们将非常感谢您给予我们五星级的反馈并根据您的体验留下积极的评价！

（14）很抱歉，我们把货发往了错误的地址，不知您是否还需要这个产品。如果需要，我们会立刻重新发货；如果不需要，我们会全额退款。

4. Translate the following letter into English.

尊敬的先生：

我们从中国驻加纳使馆商务处获得贵公司的名称及地址。兹告我公司专营工业和药物化工原料，并想同贵方建立业务联系。

为了使你们对我方产品有个全面的了解，现附上我公司经营的各种产品的全套宣传册，内有详细规格和包装情况。一收到你们的具体询价，我们马上寄样报价。

我们将以货物在装运时的质量和重量为准达成交易，而货物在出运前将由上海商检局进行检验。有关货物质量和数量等的证明将由上海商检局提供。

盼早日收到你们的回信。

中国化工产品进出口公司

经理

2018 年 11 月 15 日

5. Translate the following letter into Chinese.

Hello Customer,

Thank you for your purchase. Your package has successfully been delivered to the airline on May 14, 2018. Recently the customs is strict for parcel checking, we are speeding for you now. Please wait patiently, thanks. Hope you can receive it soon.

Best regards,

Lexi

Answers for Reference

Chapter 16   International Trade Contract Writing

16.1   Introduction

International sales and purchases are normally conducted through contracts, which are agreements reached between the seller and the buyer, concerning the establishing, modifying and terminating the rights and obligations between the two parties during a business transaction. A contract is a legal document enforceable by law and binding on the parties involved, therefore, it must be observed and implemented once the terms and conditions of the contract are reached and the document is signed between the parties. The importance of a contract can never be overstated due to this binding nature. And all the clauses of a contract must be created and reviewed carefully.

An international trading contract usually includes the following 22 provisions.

(1) Titles (名称条款).

(2) Preamble (总则条款) that covers the signing parties, date, place and parties' positions.

(3) Name of commodity (商品条款) that covers the name of the goods and specification.

(4) Quality (品质条款).

(5) Quantity (数量条款).

(6) Price(价格条款) that covers the currency for payment, unit price, total price, trade terms and inflation-proof assessment.

(7) Packing (包装条款) that covers packing way, packing weight, size and packing material.

(8) Insurance (保险条款) that covers the policy and condition of insurance.

(9) Shipment and Delivery (交货条款) that covers the delivery place, date.

(10) Industrial property right and patent (工业产权和专利条款) that covers terms of industrial property right and patent range, cost, responsibility bearing in case there is a violation to the industrial property right or patent.

(11) Payment (支付条款) that covers every detail relevant to payment making.

(12) Inspection (检验条款) that covers the testing subjects, standard, inspecting bodies, cost and authority.

(13) Training (培训条款) that covers the training program, duration, place, trainees' number and test.

(14) Confidential clause (保密条款) that sets up specific regulations for what is oriented and the confidential measures to be taken.

(15) Guarantee (保证条款) that indicates guarantee terms.

(16) Claim (索赔条款) that covers the details for claiming, for instance the conditions, the document required, the way of compensation, etc.

(17) Breach and Rescission of Contact (违约、毁约条款) that lists the terms and compensation as well as responsibility for breach and rescission of contract.

(18) Arbitration (仲裁条款) that covers details for arbitration in case of disputes.

(19) Force Majeure (不可抗力条款) that lists the causes and factors of force majeure and the settlement ways.

(20) Applicable Laws (选用法律) that indicates which laws are applied as the principal laws in case of disputes.

(21) Miscellaneous Clause (其他条款) that indicates what is unsettled in the previous clauses of the contract.

(22) Conclusion of the contract (结尾条款) that includes the signatures of the representatives of the both parties and their positions.

16.2   Writing Guide

The following are the requirements of writing a contract.

(1) The contents of contracts should conform to the principle of equality and mutual benefit and through common negotiation.

The versions of the contract are legal documents. The parties concerned are equal in legal status. Neither party has privilege to force the other party to accept its own will, so both parties should respect the other side's interests. The stipulations should be discussed by the parties concerned and reach an agreement.

(2) The stipulations of contracts should be complete, concrete, definite and without careless omissions, in order to avoid unnecessary economic losses. For example, the stipulation of shipping marks seems to be an unimportant term, but if it is indefinitely and unclearly stated, that would cause trouble when delivering the goods. Another example, the arbitration clause is the most important terms in all international trade contracts. It is not used in the execution of every contract, but if we neglect it, it will be a great problem when a dispute occurs and no agreement can be reached. When disputes occur, the foreign party directly sues to a court of their own country that throws our party into passive situation.

(3) Use words and expressions accurately, arrange the contents properly, logically and without mistakes.

The words and expressions used in the contract should not be ambiguous. For example, for the term of package we should state clearly and definitely the packing materials and ways i.e. pack in cartons, wooden cases, casks, gunny bags, etc. The expression of "ship the goods in two lots" is not complete and clear. We had better add "50% for each lot", or "60% for the first lot and the rest for the second" to the clause. These expressions are more rigorous.

16.3   Letters for Example

16.3.1   Letter One

(Sales Contract)

Seller: Oriental Trade Company

Seller's address: 56 Hainan Road, Tianjin, China

Tel: 00-00-0000000

Fax: 00-00-0000000

E-mail: orient@otc.com

Buyer: K&D CO.,LTD.

Date of signing: March 2, 2018

Signed at: Tianjin, China

Validity: 12 months

The Sales Contract is made by and between the undersigned seller and buyer whereby the seller agrees to sell and the buyer agrees to buy the under-mentioned goods according to the terms and conditions stipulated below:

(1) Name of commodity and specification: Dawei Brand Men's Shirts

(2) Quantity: 2,000 pieces

(3) Unit price: US $28.00/piece CIF Los Angeles

(4) Total value: US $56,000.00 CIF Los Angeles

(5) Packing: Each piece in a polythene bag, 40 pieces in a carton

(6) Time of shipment: July 8-10, 2018

(7) Shipment term: Partial shipment allowed; Transshipment not allowed

(8) Port of loading: Shanghai, China

(9) Port of destination: Hamburg, Germany

(10) Insurance: To be covered by the seller covering all risk for 110% of invoice value

(11) Terms of Payment: L/C at sight

The covering Letter of Credit must reach the Sellers before June 10, 2018 and is to remain valid in the above indicated loading port 15 days after the date of shipment. If the L/C fails to arrive in time, the seller reserves rights to cancel this Sale Contract and to claim from the buyer compensation for losses resulting from it.

(12) Shipping marks: At seller's option

TERMS

(1) QUALITY/QUANTITY DISCREPANCY: In case of discrepancy, claim should be filed by the buyers within 30 days after the arrival of the goods at port of destination, while for quantity discrepancy claim should be filed by the buyer within 15 days after arrival of the goods at the port of destination. In all cases, claims must be accompanied by Survey reports of recognized public surveyor agreed to by the seller. The seller shall, within 20 days after receipt of the claim, send his reply to the buyers together with suggestion for settlement.

(2) The seller reserves the option of shipping the indicated percentage more or less than the quantity hereby given in this contract, the covering Letter of Credit shall be negotiated for the amount covering the value of quantity actually shipped.

(3) The content of the covering Letter of Credit shall be in strict accordance with stipulations of the Sales Contract; in case of any variation, the buyer shall bear the expense of effecting the amendment. The seller shall not be held responsible for possible delay of shipment resulting from awaiting the amendment of the L/C, and reserve rights to claim from the buyers compensation for the losses resulting from this.

(4) Except in cases where the insurance is covered by the buyers as arranged, insurance is to be covered by the sellers with a Chinese insurance company. If insurance for additional amount or for other insurance terms is required by the buyer, Sellers should notify buyers immediately and the extra insurance premium shall be on buyers' account.

(5) INSPECTION: The Certificate of Origin and/or the Inspection Certificate of Quality/Quantity issued by China Commodity Inspection Bureau shall be taken as the basis for the shipping quality/quantity.

(6) The seller shall not be held responsible if they, owing to Force Majeure, fail to make delivery within the date stipulated in this Sales Contract or can't deliver the goods. However, the sellers shall inform the buyer immediately by fax. The seller shall deliver to the buyer by registered letter, if it is requested by the buyer, a certificate issued by the China Council for the Promotion of International Trade or by any competent authority, certifying to the existing of the said cause or causes. Buyer's failure to obtain the relative Import License is not to be treated as Force Majeure.

(7) ARBITRITION: All disputes arising in connection with the execution of the Sales Contract shall be settled amicably by negotiation. In case no settlement can be reached, the case under dispute shall then be submitted for arbitration to the Foreign Trade Arbitration Commission of the China Council for Promotion of International Trade. The decision of the Commission shall be accepted as final and binding upon both parties.

(8) LAW APPLICATION: The contract should be governed by the law of the People's Republic of China in the place where the contract is signed or the goods while the disputes arising are in the People's Republic of China or the defendant is Chinese legal person, otherwise this contract will be governed by *United Nations Convention on Contract for the International Sale of Goods*. The terms in the contract based on *INCOTERMS 2010* of the International Chamber of Commerce.

(9) This contract is made out in both Chinese and English and both of them are effective. This contract is in three copies, effective since being signed by both parties.

The Buyer: The Seller:

(Signature) (Signature)

K&D CO.,LTD. ORIENTAL TRADE COMPANY

16.3.2　Letter Two

Sales Confirmation

NO. 544

Date: November 11, 2018

Signed at: Shijiazhuang,China

The seller: China National Native Produce & Animal By-products Import and Export Corporation, Hebei Branch.

The buyer: Golden Beach CO., LTD.

The undersigned Sellers and Buyers have agreed to close the following transactions according to the terms and conditions stipulated below.

(1) Commodity: Sweet Potato Slices, FAQ.

(2) Specifications: Moisture: 20% max.

(3) Packing: All in bulk.

(4) Quantity: 18,000 metric tons with 5% more or less both in amount and quantity allowed at sellers' option.

(5) Unit Price: US $180.00 per metric ton DAT Singapore.

(6) Total Value: US $ 3,240,000.00.

(7) Time of Shipment: During December allowing partial shipment and transshipment.

(8) Port of Shipment: Tianjin.

(9) Port of Destination: Singapore.

(10) Insurance: To be covered by the sellers for 110% of the invoice value against ALL RISKS.

(11) Terms of payment: The buyers shall open with a bank acceptable to sellers an Irrevocable Sight Letter of Credit to reach the sellers 30 days before the month of shipment, valid for negotiation in China until the 15th day after the month of shipment.

(12) Commodity Inspection: It is mutually agreed that certificate of quality and weight issued by the Chinese Import and Export Commodity Inspection Bureau at the port of shipment shall be taken as the basis of delivery.

(13) Shipping Mark: At the sellers' option.

OTHER TERMS

(1) Claims if any, concerning the goods shipped shall be filed within 30 days after arrival at destination supported by an inspection report. It is understood that the sellers shall not be liable for any discrepancy of the goods shipped due to causes for which the insurance company, shipping company, other transport organization or post office are liable.

(2) All disputes arising from the execution of, or in connection with this contract, shall be settled amicably through friendly consultation. In case no settlement can be reached, the case under dispute shall then be submitted to the China International Economic and Trade Arbitration Commission of the China Council for the Promotion of International Trade (CCPIT), Beijing for arbitration in accordance with its provisional rules of procedure. The arbitral award is final and binding upon both parties.

(3) The seller shall not be responsible for late or non-delivery of goods in the event of force majeure of any contingencies beyond seller's control.

The Buyer: The Seller:

(Signature)   (Signature)

16.3.3　Letter Three

Purchase Contract

No. CFT-91020

Date: January 12, 2018

The Buyer: Cargill B.V.

The address: Capriweg4, 1044 AL Amsterdam, Netherlands

Tel: 00-00-0000000

Fax: 00-00-0000000

The Seller: Sanmenxia Fruit Juice Beverage Company

The address: Western Xiaoshan Road, San Menxia City, Hennan, China

Tel: 00-00-0000000

Fax: 00-00-0000000

Signed at: Henan, China

Validity: 12 months

This Contract is made by and between the Buyer and Seller, whereby the Buyer agrees to buy and the Seller agrees to sell the undermentioned goods subject to the terms and conditions as stipulated hereinafter:

Commodity: Frozen Concentrated Orange Juice

Brix: 65.0-66.0

Ratio: 16.0-19.0

Packing: in 260kg net/drum packaging

Price term: USD1, 130.00/MT FOB Qingdao/Tianjin

Quantity: 218.40mt (12 FCL 70 Drum/FCL)

     5% more or less tolerance in quantity acceptable

Port of destination: Rotterdam

Port of shipment: Qingdao/Tianjin

Shipment time: March-May, 2018

Document: see Appendix A

Shipment term: Partial shipment allowed; Transshipment not allowed

Payment term: D/P at sight

Force Majeure: The Seller shall not be held responsible if they, owing to Force Majeure, fail to make delivery within the date stipulated in this Sales Contract or cannot deliver the goods.

However, the Sellers shall inform the Buyer immediately by fax. The Seller shall deliver to the Buyer by registered letter, if it is requested by the Buyer, a certificate issued by the China Council for the Promotion of International Trade or by any competent authority, certifying to the existing of the said cause or causes.

Appendix Documents: the appendix documents in this contract is an important part of the whole contract.

Arbitration terms: see Appendix B

Buyer: Seller:

(Signature)   (Signature)

Cargill B.V.   Sanmenxia Fruit Juice Beverage Company

16.4 Word and Phrases

1. **implement** *v.* put into effect or carry out 履行；实施
2. **overstate** *v.* express or state strongly 强调
3. **stipulate** *v.* state clearly and firmly as a requirement 讲明；规定
4. **privilege** *n.* special right or advantage only to a particular person, class or rank or the

holder of a certain position   特有的权利、利益或好处

5. **ambiguous**   *adj.*   uncertain in meaning or intention   意向不明
6. **rigorous**   *adj.*   strictly accurate or detailed   精确的；严密的
7. **discrepancy**   *n.*   difference or failure to agree   差异；不符；不一致
8. **FCL (full container load)**   一整集装箱；整柜
9. **hereinafter**   *adv.*   in a subsequent part of this socument or statement or matter   下文
10. **amicable**   *adj.*   show friendliness; without hostility   友好的；无敌意的
11. **violation**   *n.*   violating or being violated   违背；违反
12. **terms and conditions**   条款
13. **equality and mutual benefit**   平等互利
14. **on one's account**   由某人来付款
15. **registered letter**   挂号信
16. **Import License**   进口许可证
17. **shipping marks**   唛头
18. **negotiation**   *n.*   议付
19. **by-product**   *n.*   a product mode during the manufacture of something else   副产品

16.5　Notes

1. **inflation-proof assessment**   保值
2. **Breach and Rescission of Contract**   违约；毁约
3. **Miscellaneous Clause**   其他条款
4. **Force Majeure**   不可抗力
5. **submit for arbitration**   提交仲裁
6. **China Council for the Promotion of International Trade**   中国国际贸易促进委员会
7. **Frozen Concentrated Orange Juice**   冷藏浓缩橘汁

16.6　Useful Expressions

1. In case of discrepancy, claim should be filed by the Buyers within 30 days after the arrival of the goods at port of destination.

当发生矛盾时，索赔须于货物到达目的口岸之日起 30 天内由买方提出。

2. The Seller agrees to sell the under-mentioned goods subject to the terms and conditions as stipulated hereinafter.

卖方同意按下述的合同条款和条件出售下述商品。

3. The seller shall, within 20 days after receipt of the claim, send his reply to the Buyers together with suggestion for settlement.

卖方应在收到索赔申请之日起 20 日内答复买方，并给出解决问题的建议。

4. The contract of the covering Letter of Credit shall be in strict accordance with stipulations of the Sales Contract.

本合同项下的信用证应该严格遵守销售合同的规定。

5. The Buyer shall bear the expense of effecting the amendment.

买方应承担修改信用证的费用。

6. The decision of the Commission shall be accepted as final and binding on both parties.

委员会的决定是最终的，对双方均有约束力。

7. The Seller shall not be held responsible if they, owing to Force Majeure, fail to make delivery within the date stipulated in this Sales Contract or can not deliver the goods.

因不可抗力致使卖方未能在销售合同规定的时间内交货或不能交货的，卖方可以免责。

16.7   Exercises

1. Answer the following questions.

(1) What does an international trading contract usually include?

(2) What is the main requirement of writing a contract?

2. Discuss on the following topic.

Some experts of commercial law in the USA and Europe call for a reform in the writing of legal documents and advocate the use of simple words and everyday language. As a learner of English as a second language, what is your idea in drafting a business contract?

3. Translate the following clauses from a sales contract into English.

（1）本合同项下的货物装船前在装货港由中国商品检验局检验，该商检局出具的质量和数量证明书将是最终的，对双方均有约束力。

（2）如果发现质量或数量与合同、发票或质量证书不符，买方有权根据中国商检局出具的检验证书在目的港卸货后 90 天内向卖方提出索赔。赔偿责任属于船公司或保险公司的情况除外。

（3）若出现争议，双方应友好协商解决，协商不成可提交中国海事仲裁委员会仲裁。

（4）如果由于卖方没有及时通知而造成买方未能及时办理保险，卖方将承担责任。

（5）责任方应尽可能地将发生的不可抗力事故的情况以电传的形式通知对方，并于 14 天内以航空挂号信形式将有关当局出具的证明文件交予另一方确认。

（6）本合同的附录 1～9 为本合同不可分割的组成部分，与合同正文具有同等效力。

4. Translate the following clauses from a sales contract into Chinese.

(1) The Contract is signed by the representatives of both parties on March 2, 2018, in Zhengzhou, Henan Province, the People's Republic of China. After signing the Contract, both parties shall apply to their respective Government Authorities for approval. The date of approval last obtained shall be taken as the date of effectiveness of the Contract. Both parties shall exert their best efforts to obtain the approval within 60 days and inform the other party by telex and thereafter confirm the same by letter. If the Contract can not come into effect within 6 months from the date of signing the Contract, the Contract shall be binding neither on party A, nor the party B.

(2) All disputes arising from the execution of, or in connection with the Contract shall be settled through friendly consultation between the parties. In case no settlement can be reached, the dispute shall be submitted for arbitration. The arbitration shall take place in Beijing, China and shall be conducted by the Foreign Economic and Trade Arbitration Commission of the China Council for the Promotion of International Trade in accordance with its rules and procedures. The arbitration decision shall be final and binding on both parties.

5. Write a sales contract with information gathered from the following correspondences.

ABC TRADING COMPANY LIMITED

1) Incoming letter

July 18, 2018

ABC Trading Company Limited

Shenzhen, China

Dear Sirs,

　　One of our clients in London wants to buy a parcel of 3,000 dozen of Ladies' Blouses. We would therefore ask you to make us an offer based on CIF London including our commission of 3%.

　　We shall appreciate it deeply if you can arrange for shipment to be made as early as possible by direct steamer for London.

　　As usual, our sight irrevocable L/C will be opened in your favor 30 days before the time of shipment.

Yours faithfully,

CDE TRADING CO., LTD.

---

2) Outgoing letter

August 6, 2018

CDE Trading Co., Ltd.

London, England

Dear Sirs,

　　Thank you for your letter of July 18 inquiring for 3,000 dozen Ladies' Blouses.

　　We are glad in making you an offer as follows, subject to your acceptance reaching here not later than August 183,000 dozen of Art. No.108 Ladies' Blouses in pink, blue and yellow colors, equally assorted, with the size assortment of S/3, M/6, and L/3 per dozen, packed in cantons, at USD 36.00 per dozen CIFC 3% London, for shipment from any China's port in October.

Please note that, since there is no direct steamer available for London in October, we find it only possible to ship the parcel with transshipment at Tokyo.

We look forward to your early reply.

Yours faithfully,
ABC TRADING COMPANY LIMITED

3) Incoming Letter

August 19, 2018

ABC Trading Company Limited

Shenzhen, China

Dear Sirs,

Thank you for your letter of August 6 offering us 3,000 dozen of Ladies' Blouses at USD 36.00 per dozen CIFC 3% London.

We are happy to tell you that we have succeed to persuade our clients to accept your price, though they found it a little high. We are now arranging with our bank for the relevant L/C.

When making the shipment, kindly see to it that insurance is to be effected against All Risks and War Risk for 110% of the invoice value. As to the shipping mark, we will notify you as soon as possible.

Yours faithfully,

Answers for Reference

Chapter 17   Contracts and Agreements

17.1   Introduction

International business is much more complicated than domestic business, thus contracts are indispensable. It may be formal or informal. The business contract which is generally adopted in international trade activity is the formal written one. Should any conflict between the two sides arise later, reference is generally made to the contract in the effort to resolve the misunderstanding. The common forms of contracts are formal contract, confirmation, agreement, and memorandum.

It is easy to tell the difference between an agreement and a contract. First, in terms of the content, an agreement usually focuses on the principle, on which further discussion will be conducted; while a contract focuses on specific items based on the principle that concerned both sides have concluded. In another word, an agreement draws an outline for a program and functions as a base for a contract, while a contract is with details and usually based on the agreement made before.

Comparing their range the two cover respectively, we can see a contract is concentrated on only one item while an agreement may often carry or include several contracts. For instance, a trade agreement is only the master contract of a projection, and it includes several appended documents. After an agreement being signed, several specific contracts can be worked on and made. But some contracts are made right after negotiation if it is not related to complex business.

17.2   Writing Guide

Contracts or agreements don't have fixed forms. In practice, complete and valid contracts or agreements usually consists of three parts: HEAD, BODY and END.

1. The HEAD

The head covers the following contents.

(1) The title of the contract or agreement, e.g. Purchase Contract, Agency Agreement, Exclusive Sales Agreement, etc. The title indicates the character of the contract or agreement.

(2) The number of the contract or agreement.

(3) The date and the place of signing the contract or agreement (some contracts or agreements put the date and the place in the END).

(4) The preface of the contract or agreement. In the preface, there are the parties' names which state clearly the Sellers and the Buyers, explain the principles and the purposes of signing the contract or agreement (many contracts only mention the parties' names) .

2. The BODY

The body is the most important part in the contract or agreement. We may use the style of stipulation or the style of forms or we may combine the two styles together to state clearly the contents negotiated by the parties concerned. The stipulations in international trade contracts have been mentioned in last chapter. The contents of other contracts and agreements are complicated. The terms and conditions are different. But they have certain forms. When we write them, we can consult example versions.

3 .The END

The contents in this part usually include the copies and the conservation of the contract or agreement, and the seals affixed by the parties, etc. If the contract or agreement is accompanied by some enclosures, we should state clearly the names of the enclosures as well as the number of the copies as the integral part of the whole contract.

The requirement of writing contracts and agreements is the same as writing international trade contracts which we have mentioned last chapter.

17.3   Letters for Example

17.3.1   Letter One

(Contract of Coca-Cola Soft Drinks on Consignment)

Contract No. [2018]310

Beijing, P.R. of China

Date: April 4, 2018

Consignee: China National Cereals, Oils and Foodstuffs Import and Export Corporation (hereinafter called Party A)

Consigner: Coca-Cola in China (hereinafter called Party B)

Party B and party A on consignment basis, subject to terms and conditions as stipulated below:

1. Name of Commodity: Coca-Cola Soft Drinks

2. Quantity: 20,000 cases/cartons (15,000 cases in bottles, 5,000 cartons in cans)

---

3. Specifications: A. Bottles: 24×65 oz. Bottles per case

B. Cans: 25×12 oz. Cans per carton

4. Unit Price: A. Bottles: US $ 240 per case Franco Wagon Shenzhen

B. Cans: US $100 per can Franco Wagon Shenzhen

5. Total Value: USD 4,100,000

6. Time of Shipment: July, 2018

7. Destination:

Beijing, 10,000 cases/carton (of which 7,000 cases in bottles and 3,000 cartons in cans.)

Guangdong, 7,000 cases/cartons (of which 5,000 cases in bottles and 2,000 cartons in cans.)

Shanghai, 3,000 cases

8. Insurance:

Party A shall keep the goods insured at the full wholesale list price against damage or destruction, and loss of very kind while the goods are in the possession of party A. Party A shall cause party B to be a beneficiary of such insurance together with consignee, as each party's respective interests appear. Party A shall provide Party B a copy of the current insurance policies, on request.

9. Documents:

Immediately after the shipment is effected, Party B shall notify Party A by Fax and Cable of the shipped quantity, number of cases, and Bill of Lading number, and air-mail to Party A the clean-on-board Bill of Lading and Commercial Invoice in quintuplicate.

10. Terms and Conditions:

A. The contract shall be effective for 6 months (180 days) starting from the goods' arrival at the destination.

B. The location, methods and prices for selling shall be decided by Party A according to specific situation. However, Party B has the right to make proposals in this respect. Both parties should exchange information in a timely way, study together, and settle problems that may arise during the consignment period. What's more, party B shall facilitate sales in every possible way.

C. If any breakage of container is found at the goods' arrival for which Party B is responsible for, or any deterioration of quality occurs during the period of consignment, Party B shall make compensation at the contracted prices or replace the substandard goods with fresh goods against Party A's certificate.

11. Terms of Payment:

A. Party A shall, within 15 days after the expiration of the period of consignment (180 days), remit the total amount to Party B at the contract unit prices according to the varieties and quantities actually sold.

B. For unsold goods, Party A shall make a list to Party B. The two parties shall decide through mutual consultations, whether to return the unsold goods to Party B or to automatically transfer them to the next consignment contract.

C. The price of the portion of the shipment suffering quality deterioration or breakage shall be deducted from the total amount to be remitted, with the exception of those already disposed of or settled. However, Party A must furnish Party B with detailed invoice of deductions.

12. This contract is made out in Chinese and English and both versions are equally valid.

CONSIGNEE(Party A) Seal :   CONSIGNER(pParty B) Seal:

17.3.2　Letter Two

(Exclusive Agency Agreement)

This agreement is made and entered into by and between the parties concerned on January 20, 2018 in China on the basis of equality and mutual benefit to develop business on terms and conditions mutually agreed upon as follows:

1. The Parties Concerned

Party A(supplier): Qingdao Hongda Industrial Co., Ltd.

　　　　　　Add: 25 Qutangxia Road, Qingdao, China

　　　　　　Tel: 000000　　　Fax: 000000

Party B(agent): Huaxing Trading Company Ltd.

　　　　　　Add: 126 Waterloo Street, Singapore 0718

　　　　　　Te: 000000 Fax: 000000

2. Appointment

Party A hereby appoints Party B as its Exclusive Agent to solicit order for the commodity stipulated in Article 3 from customers in the territory stipulated in Article 4, and Party B accepts and assumes such appointment.

3. Commodity

"Golden Fish" Brand Washing Machines

4. Territory

SINGAPORE

5. Minimum Turnover

It is mutually agreed that party B shall undertake to solicit order for the aforesaid commodity from customers for not less than USD 100,000.00 in the above territory during the effective period of this agreement.

6. Price and Payment

The price for each individual transaction shall be fixed through negotiation between Party B and the buyer, and subject to Party A's final confirmation.

Payment shall be made by confirmed, irrevocable L/C opened by the buyer in favor of Party A, which shall reach Party A 15 days before the date of shipment.

7. Exclusive Rights

In consideration of the exclusive rights granted herein, Party A shall not, directly or indirectly, sell or export the commodity stipulated in Article 4 to customers in Singapore through channel other than Party B; Party B shall not sell, distribute or promote the sales of any products competitive with or similar to the above commodity in Singapore and shall not solicit or accept orders for the purpose of selling them outside Singapore. Party A shall refer to Party B any inquiries or orders for the commodity in question received by Party A from other firms in Singapore during the validity of this agreement.

8. Market Report

Party B shall have the obligation to forward once every three months Party A detailed report on current market condition and of consumer's comments, and if there's any special change in the market, Party B shall also report timely to Party A its full particulars in writing. Party B shall also supply Party A with quotations and advertising materials on similar products of other suppliers.

9. Advertising and Expenses

Party A shall bear all expenses for advertising and publicity in connection with the commodity in question in Singapore within validity of this agreement, and shall submit to Party A all audio and video materials intended for advertising for prior approval.

10. Commission

Party A shall pay Party B a commission of 5% on the net invoiced selling price on all orders directly obtained by Party B and accepted by Party A. No commission shall be paid until Party A receives the full payment for each order.

11. Transactions between Governmental Bodies

Transactions concluded between governmental bodies of Party A and Party B shall not be restricted by the terms and conditions of this agreement. Nor shall be the amount of such transactions counted as part of the turnover stipulated in Article 5.

12. Industrial Property Rights

Party B may use the trade-marks owned by Party A for the sale of the Washing Machines covered herein within the validity of this agreement, and shall acknowledge that all patents, trademarks, copy rights or any other industrial property rights used or embodied in the Washing Machine shall remain to be the sole properties of Party A. Should any infringement be found, Party B shall promptly notify and assist Party A to take steps to protect the latter's rights.

13. Validity of Agreement

This agreement, when duly signed by the both parties concerned, shall remain in force for 12 months from February 1, 2018 to November 30, 2018 and it shall be extended for another 12 months upon expiration unless notice in writing is given to the contrary.

14. Termination

During the validity of this agreement, if either of the two parties is found to have violated the stipulations herein, the other party has right to terminate the agreement.

15. Force Majeure

Either party shall not be held responsible for failure or delay to perform all or any part of this agreement due to flood, fire, earthquake, drought, war or any other events which could not be predicted, controlled, avoided or overcome by the relative party. However, the party affected by the event of Force Majeure shall inform the other party of its occurrence in writing as soon as possible and thereafter sends a certificate of the event issued by the relevant authorities to the other party within 15 days after its occurrence.

16. Arbitration

All disputes arising from the performance of this agreement shall be settled through friendly negotiation. Should no settlement be reached through negotiation, the case shall then be submitted for arbitration to the China International Economic and Trade Arbitration Commission and the rules of this Commission shall be applied. The result of the arbitration shall be final and binding or both parties.

Party A: Qingdao Hongda
Industrial Co., Ltd.
(Signature)

Party B: Huaxing Trading
Company (Pte).
(Signature)

17.3.3　Letter Three

(Consignment Agreement)

This agreement is made between ABC Co. (hereinafter referred to as the Consignor), having its registered office at New York and XYZ Co. (hereinafter referred to as the Consignee), having its registered office at Nanjing Road, Shanghai, China on the following terms and conditions.

1. The Consignor shall ship the computers to the consignee on Consignment basis at the prevailing international market prices on CIF terms from time to time. The interval between each shipment shall be approximately 90 days.

2. The Consignee must try to sell the consignments at the best possible prices after obtaining the approval of the Consignor as to price, terms, etc.

3. Each shipment by ship at the initial stage will not exceed USD 200,000.00 only and the outstanding liabilities on the Consignee shall be in the vicinity of no more than USD 100,000.00 only.

4. The Consignor shall at no time be responsible for any bad debts arising from sales to any buyers. Making payments to the Consignor shall at all times be the sole responsibility of the Consignee.

5. The Consignee shall accept the Bills of Exchange drawn by the Consignor on him at 90 days' sight with interest payable at 3% per annum.

6. The Consignee shall collect the shipping documents including B/L from the Consignor's bank against Trust Receipt duly signed by the consignee.

7. The Consignor shall absorb insurance premium and warehousing charges up to the date of delivery to customers.

8. The Consignor shall observe the regulations of the government of China.

9. This Agreement is made out in both Chinese and English and both of them are effective. This agreement is in three copies, effective since being signed by both parties.

As a token of acceptance, both parties have set their respective hands on this July 25, 2018 with the knowledge of the contents stated hereinabove.

ABC Co:_____ XYZ Co:_____
(Signature) (Signature)

17.4　Words and Phrases

1. **indispensable**　*adj.*　absolutely essential　必需的；不可缺少的

2. **memorandum**　*n.*　note made for future use　记录；备忘录

3. **append**　*v.*　attach or add sth.　附加、添上或增补某事物

4. **projection**　*n.*　thing that is projected, esp. a mental image viewed as reality　（制定的）规划；（尤指）设想；设计

5. **deteriorate**　v.　become worse in quality or condition　变坏；变质；恶化

6. **bear**　v.　take(responsibility, etc); shoulder　负起；肩负

7. **turnover**　*n.*　amount of business done by a company with a certain period of time　（一定时期的）营业额

8. **solicit**　*v.*　try to obtain　设法获得（某事物）

9. **affix**　*v.*　stick, fasten or attach sth.　黏上；贴上；附上

10. **deduct**　v.　take away　减去；扣除

11. **infringement**　*n.*　infringing or being infringed　违反；触犯；侵害

12. **violate**　*v.*　break or be contrary to (a rule, principle, treaty, etc)　违反；违背（规则、原则、条约等）

13. **with the exception of**　除……之外

14. **in consideration of**　基于

15. **intend for**　打算供……使用

17.5　Notes

1. **24×65 oz. bottles per case**　每箱 24 瓶，每瓶 65 盎司

2. **clean-on-board Bill of Lading**　清洁的已装船提单

3. **outstanding liabilities**　未履行的义务

4. **Trust Receipt**　信托收据

17.6　Useful Expressions

1. Both parties should exchange information in a timely way, study together, and settle any problems that may arise during the consignment period while Party B shall facilitate sales in every possible way.

双方应定期交换信息、共同学习并及时解决任何可能发生在交货期间的问题，同时，乙方应促进各种可能途径的销售。

2. If any breakage of container is found at the goods' arrival for which Party B is responsible, or any deterioration of quality occurs during the period of consignment, Party B shall make compensation at the contracted prices or replace the substandard goods with fresh goods against Party A's certificate.

如果集装箱的破损是在货物到达时被发现，应由乙方负责，或者交货期内商品出现了变质，乙方应按合同价格补偿或者依据甲方证明用新鲜商品更换不合格产品。

3. This contract is made out in the original in Chinese and English; each party keeps one of them and both versions are equally valid.

本合同原文用中文和英文两种文字表示；各方分持一份，两份文本具有同等效力。

4. This agreement is made and entered into by and between the parties concerned on January 20, 2018, China, on the basis of equality and mutual benefit to develop business on terms and conditions mutually agreed upon as follows:

本协议由双方当事人于 2018 年 1 月 20 日在中国订立，双方在平等互利的基础上开展业务并按约定确定的合同条款如下。

5. Party A hereby appoints Party B as its Exclusive Agent to solicit order for the commodity stipulated in Article 3 from customers in the territory stipulated in Article 4, and Party B accepts and assumes such appointment.

甲方指定乙方为其独家代理，为第三条所列商品从第四条所列区域的顾客招揽订单，乙方接受上述委任。

6. Party B shall not sell, distribute or promote the sales of any products competitive with or similar to the above commodity in Singapore and shall not solicit or accept orders for the purpose of selling them outside Singapore. Party A shall refer to Party B any inquiries or orders for the commodity in question received by Party A from other firms in Singapore during the validity of this agreement.

乙方不得在新加坡销售、分销或促销任何与上述商品有竞争的或类似的商品，不得招揽或接受拟卖给新加坡以外的订单。本协议有效期内，甲方从新加坡其他公司收到的有关商品的询价或订单应转告乙方。

7. Either of party shall not be held responsible for failure or delay to perform all or any part of this agreement due to flood, fire, earthquake, drought, war or any other events which could not be predicted, controlled, avoided or overcome by the relative party.

由于水灾、火灾、地震、干旱、战争或协议一方无法预见、控制、避免或克服的其他事件导致不能或者暂时不能全部或者部分履行本协议，该方不负责任。

8. The Consignee shall collect the shipping documents including B/L from the Consignor's bank against Trust Receipt duly signed by the Consignee.

代售人以签字信托收据从寄售人银行换取包括提单在内的装运单据。

17.7　Exercise

1. Answer the following question.

What are main differences between Contract and Agreement?

2. Discuss on the following topic.

Agency and Consignment are two modes of international trade. They are more and more popular in the international trade. You can discuss about their advantages and disadvantages and give some advice on how to use it better.

3. Translate the following sentences into English.

（1）由于水灾、火灾、地震、干旱、战争或其他一方无法预测、无法控制、无法避免和克服的其他事件不能或暂时不能全部或部分履行本协议，该方不负责任。

（2）本合同其他条款如与本附加条款有抵触时，以本附加条款为准（本附加条款有效并有约束力）。

（3）代售人在获得寄售人对价格、条款的许可之后，必须尽力以最好的价格出售寄售商品，但寄售人对赊销造成的坏账不负任何责任。

（4）甲方指定乙方为独家代理，在北美地区销售青岛啤酒。乙方有义务不遗余力地按照甲方规定的价格进行促销。

（5）本协议有效期内，甲方应将其收到的来自德国其他商家的有关代理产品的询价或订单转交给乙方。

4. Translate the following part of an agreement into Chinese.

This agreement is made and entered into this first day of March 2013 between the AA plant, Bamako (hereinafter called Party A) and Mr. Lang Ming (hereinafter called Party B).

Whereas Party A is willing to employ Party B and Party B agrees to work as Party A's engineer in Bamako, it is hereby mutually agreed as follows.

(1) The employment is for a period of two years from July 1, 2015 to June 30, 2017, exactly functioning from the date Party B arrives at the AA Plant and he will return to his country when he completes his two years service.

(2) Party B's monthly salary is USD 2,000.00 which shall be paid monthly in Bamako and can be remitted to China at the direction of Party B. Party B's housing shall be provided by Party A during the service period.

(3) Party B shall be provided by Party A with the air tickets from Guangzhou to Bamako, and from Bamako to Guangzhou upon terminating the service.

(4) Party B shall obey the laws and regulations of Mali.

(5) This Agreement is made both in English language and Chinese language in duplicate, each of which shall be signed and kept by either party.

5. Write a business contract according to the particulars given below.

卖方：中国粮食食品进出口公司
买方：韩国仁川粮食食品贸易公司
商品：中国东北大米
规格：一级
数量：20 公吨
单价：每公吨成本加运费到仁川价格 300 美元/千克
总值：60 000 美元
包装：麻袋包，每袋净重 100 千克
交货期：2018 年 6 月份
装卸港：由大连至仁川
保险：由买方投保
付款条件：买方开立以卖方为受益人的不可撤销信用证，卖方凭跟单汇票向开证行议付。
签约地点和日期：2018 年 3 月 5 日于北京
合同号：BDW201

Answers for Reference

Chapter 18　Other Letters Writing

18.1　Introduction

In this chapter, we will introduce some other business letters writing including Fax, E-mail, job application, resume, and resignation letter.

Fax in communications is the transmission of still image by wire or radio. A fax transmitter scans a document and produces electrical signals that are sent to a fax receiver, which produces a copy of document. Fax equipment is used when a copy of document has to be transmitted rapidly from one place to another. It is used to send weather maps, charts, newspaper proof pages, X-ray photos, order forms, bank documents, finger prints, identification photos, other documents and papers.

Electronic mail (E-mail), widely used in modern business circles, refers to computer-based system whereby one computer sends a message to another. Since computers can store data, an incoming message is filed in an electronic "mail-box". A private electronic "mail-box" means that only the intended recipients can read their own mail.

Fax and E-mail are two modern communication services which can send a message to any person very quickly in the world. They have following advantages.

(1) They can be communicated as fast as telex and an international telephone.

(2) They are cheaper than telex and international telephone.

(3) They are 24 hours service and the message can be received unattended.

When applying for employment by E-mail, a job application letter usually accompanies with a resume. In many situations, an employer may be flooded by a stack of a hundred or more resumes, and getting an interview represents a major break-through. An excellent letter of application doesn't guarantee a position necessarily, but it does insure consideration and a better chance of an interview.

There are two kinds of application letters.

(1) Solicited application letter is a letter written in response to an announced job opening. If you send a solicited application letter, you know what qualifications the organization is seeking from the advertisement. But you may have many competitors competing for the same job or position because they have seen the advertisement too. So you must give more emphases on your qualifications to catch the reader's attention.

(2) Unsolicited application letter is a letter sent to an organization that has not announced an opening. In sending an unsolicited application letter, you stand a better chance of getting individualized attention since there are fewer or no competitors. You must know the needs of the employer and focus on the needs.

Resumes usually display a rather simple table of data depicting your past work history and educational background. It should highlight your accomplishments to show a potential employer that you are qualified for the work you want. And it is not a biography of everything you have done.

18.2   Writing Guide

There is no standard format for resume. Generally speaking, a resume should consist of six parts.

(1) Heading (Resume)

(2) Contact Information (name, telephone number, address)

(3) Work Objective

(4) Education (degree, major, schools, major course, special training)

(5) Special Skills (foreign language, computer application)

(6) Honor or Awards

(7) Work Experience

Resumes sent through the mail are normally accompanied by an application letter. One should avoid overwhelming a one-page resume with a two-page letter or repeating the contents of the resume in the letter. A short and succinct one-page letter which highlights one or two points in the resume is sufficient. An application should include four components.

(1) Purposes of writing (job vacancy and its information source)

(2) Qualification (highlight one's value to the employers)

(3) Request for the interview

(4) Enclosure/Contact information (address, telephone number)

A good resume or application letter should be effective in three respects.

1) Content

You should offer the information closely related to the employer's needs to convince the employer that you are the right person for the job. When stating the accomplishments, you'd better use facts and figures that are more convincing.

2) Language

The language you use should be direct, concise and positive. It can make ourselves understood very well. Before it is delivered, we should carefully check spelling, grammar and punctuation, because a misspelling or misuse of punctuation may lead to a failure in a job-hunting.

3) Layout

You should state your strongest points to the starting places to attract employer's attention. For example, in the resume of a graduate, the "education" section should be put first and the performance in the university is the focus. In addition, you should arrange the structure of your resume or application to make them well organized and professional.

18.3　Letters for Example

18.3.1　Letter One

(Example of Fax)

F. Lynch & Co., Ltd.

(Head Office), Nesson House, Newell Street, Birmingham B3 3EL

Tel: 000000 Fax: 000000 Telex: 000000

FAX MESSAGE

Page 1/1

Message for: D. Jesus

From: L Navarro

Address: Satex S.P.A., Via di pietra, 0016 Roma

Date: September 2, 2018

Fax number: (06) 4815472

Dear Mr. Jesus,

This is an urgent request for a consignment to replace the damaged delivery that we received, and of which you have already been informed.

Please airfreight the following items:

Cat. No:	Quantity
RN30	50
Ag20	70
L26	100

The damaged consignment will be returned to you on receipt of the replacement.

Yours sincerely,

(Signed)

18.3.2　Letter Two

(Example of E-mail)

From: Wang Lingling, General Manager
To: Sam Smith, General Manager
Date: Tuesday, July 4, 2018
Subject: Letter of Credit NO. 345

Dear Mr. Smith,

Your Letter of Credit No.345 covering your Order No.123 for 40 metric tons of Ore has reached us this morning. Thank you.

After reading it thoroughly, we found that there was no stipulation of partial shipments being allowed in the relative L/C, so we can hardly manage to arrange this parcel. When making our offer No.234 dated February 5, 2018, we stated clearly that the parcel was to be divided into 2 lots. That is: 20 metric tons for each.

At present, the first lot of the goods is ready for shipment, so we have to request you to amend the L/C accordingly as soon as possible.

Yours faithfully,

(Signed)

General Manager

18.3.3　Letter Three

(Example of Job Application)

Dear Sir/Madam:

Your advertisement for a Network Maintenance Engineer in the April 10 *Student Daily* interested me because the position that you described sounds exactly like the kind of job I am seeking.

According to the advertisement, your position requires top University Bachelor or above in Computer Science or equivalent field who is proficient in Windows NT4.0 and LINUX System. I feel that I am competent to meet the requirements. I will be graduating from Tsinghua University this year with a M.S. degree. My studies have included courses in computer control and management. In addition, I designed a control simulation system developed with Microsoft Visual InterDev and SQL Server.

My school report can prove that I have mastered the principle of my major and skills of practice.

I would appreciate your time in reviewing my enclosed resume and if there is any additional information you require, please contact me. My telephone number is 1398****451. I would welcome an opportunity for a personal interview.

Yours sincerely,

(Signed)

18.3.4　Letter Four

(Example of Job Application)

Personal Data:

Name: Tony

Gender: Male

Data of birth: November 11, 1987

Email: ****** @msn.com

Phone: 158******8888

Fax: 027-12345678

Address: Room 34, NO 123, Hangzhou Street, Wuhan 430000

Objective:

A managerial assistant in Human Resource Management

Education:

2007.9-2011.6, Ocean University of China, Business Management

2011.9-present, Beijing University, Law

Main courses:

Management of Human Resources

Managerial Communication

Management Information

International Business and Trade

Corporative Law

Skills:

Excellent written and spoken English skills

Skilled in use of Windows/Office/SAP

Certificate:

CET6 (627)

BEC Van

National Computer Rank Examination Certificate (Grade 3)

Practice:

2008.6-2008.8, Assistant of an HR Manager in CEMEX(Tianjin) Co., LTD.

Duties: Help the manager to put files in order, recruit persons and organize activities.

18.3.5 Letter Five

(Example of Resignation Letter)

Dear Jacky,

    I regret to tell you that I have decided to resign from my present position as your assistant from November 11.

    Thank you for giving me a chance to accept the training of SAP7.2 and your guidance. I gained valuable experience in this company. I hope my resignation would not cause you much inconvenience.

    Thank you for taking care of me for many years. I would appreciate it if you could provide me a reference letter.

                                       Yours sincerely,

                                       (Signed)

18.4 Words and Phrases

1. **scan** *v.* pass an electronic beam over(sth) 扫描

2. **succinct** *adj.* expressed briefly and clearly; concise 简明的；简洁的

3. **proficient** *adj.* doing or able to do sth. in a skilled or an expert way because of training and practice 精通的；熟练的

4. **resume** *n.* brief account of someboby's previous career 简历；履历

5. **recipient** *n.* person who receives sth. 接收者

6. **convince** *v.* make sb. feel certain; cause sb. to realize 使某人确信；使某人明白

7. **punctuation** (art, practice or system of)punctuating 标点符号的使用；标点符号的用法

8. **equivalent** *adj.* equal in value, amount, meaning, importance, etc. （价值、数量、意义、重要性等）相同的

9. **shape** *v.* have a great influence on (sb. or sth.); determine the nature of (sth.) 对（某人或某物）有重大影响；决定某事物的性质

10. **vacancy** *n.* unfiled position or post 空处；空位；空缺；

18.5 Notes

1. **team-oriented** 具有团队精神

2. **Work Objective**　招聘职位

3. **Honor or Awards**　荣誉或奖励

4. **M.S. (the short form for Master of Science)**　理科硕士

5. **Human Resource Management**　人力资源管理

18.6　Useful Expressions

1. The damaged consignment will be returned to you on receipt of the replacement.

损坏的货物在收到替换品后将归还给你方。

2. Your Letter of Credit No.345 covering your Order No.123 for 40 metric tons of Ore has reached us this morning.

今天早上你方第 123 号订单项下 40 公吨矿石的第 345 号信用证已经到达我处。

3. Your advertisement for a Network Maintenance Engineer in the April 10 *Student Daily* interested me because the position that you described sounds exactly like the kind of job I am seeking.

贵公司在 4 月 10 日《学生日报》上刊登的招聘网络维护工程师的广告对我有很大的吸引力，这正是我梦寐以求的工作。

4. I would appreciate your time in reviewing my enclosed resume and if there is any additional information you require, please contact me. I would welcome an opportunity for a personal interview.

如能在百忙之中抽时间看看我随信附寄的简历将不胜感激。如您还需要什么材料，请告之。非常希望给我一次面试的机会。

18.7　Exercises

1. Answer the following questions.

(1) What advantages do Fax and E-mails have?

(2) What parts does a resume mainly include?

(3) What should we pay attention to in writing a resume or job application?

2. Discuss on the following topic.

"Your resume is scanned, not read." Most employers are busy people who normally may glance at a resume for only 10 to 20 seconds; therefore it is important to catch their attention. If you are a graduate, how will you successfully obtain a personal interview?

3. Translate the following information into E-mail message.

此信专为询问贵公司今秋产品。

去年贵公司产品设计新颖，深受我店顾客欢迎且销售甚好。圣诞将至，房屋装饰又会像往常一样在圣诞节前成为热潮，由于贵公司一向供货及时、质量上乘，我们仍有意向贵方订货。

但我们欲先对贵方产品有所了解再下订单。望寄来附有产品图片的最新产品目录。

注：（收件人、发件人、发件日期和邮件地址可自行选择）

4. Translate the following letter into Chinese.

Dear Sir:

Do you have a position for a part-time secretary in your company? I am able to work from noon to evening.

As a graduate of English literature from Wuhan University, I am able to write letters and reports in English. I have attended several meetings and seminars on behalf of the company to present products to potential customers.

I have always admired your company and should welcome an opportunity of becoming associated with it. My previous employer will ensure you of my competency and dependability. If there is a vacancy, may an interview be arranged on me?

Yours sincerely,

(Signed)

---

5. Write an application letter according to the following information.

(1) Ms. Wang, a partner with Tianjin office, who informed you that the Guangzhou office of the company is seeking to hire quality individuals for auditor program.

(2) You have three years of accounting experience, including interning as an auditor last year with the Tianjin office of CA. You will receive your MBA this June from Peking University.

(3) You will be in the Guangzhou area the week of May 21.

······· **Answers for Reference** ·······

参 考 文 献

[1] 石定乐，蔡蔚. 实用商务英语写作[M]. 2 版. 北京：北京理工大学出版社，2006.

[2] 张爱玲. 外贸英文制单[M]. 2 版. 北京：首都经济贸易大学出版社，2013.

[3] 汪琦. 国际贸易单证实务[M]. 北京：中国纺织出版社，2009.

[4] 黄晶晶. 外贸单证理论与实务[M]. 天津：天津大学出版社，2013.

[5] 于晓云. 外贸函电[M]. 北京：首都经济贸易大学出版社，2015.

[6] 王妍，刘亚卓. 外贸函电[M]. 2 版. 北京：北京大学出版社，2013.

[7] 梁树新. 外贸函电情景实训[M]. 北京：清华大学出版社，2014.

[8] 王建培. 外贸函电专业英语[M]. 武汉：武汉大学出版社，2011.

[9] 诸葛霖，王燕希. 外贸英文书信[M]. 3 版. 北京：对外经济贸易大学出版社，2007.

[10] 杨晋. 现代国际商务函电[M]. 天津：天津大学出版社，2007.

[11] 蔡惠伟. 外经贸函电教程[M]. 上海：华东理工大学出版社，2007.

[12] 黄丽威. 外贸函电与单证[M]. 北京：高等教育出版社，2006.

[13] 王朝晖. 实用外贸英语谈判与函电[M]. 北京：对外经济贸易大学出版社，2006.

[14] 闫兴伯，黄宪西. 商务英语函电[M]. 2 版. 北京：高等教育出版社，2001.

[15] 石定乐，蔡蔚. 实用商务英语写作[M]. 2 版. 北京：北京理工大学出版社，2006.

[16] 顾乾毅. 国际商贸英语[M]. 广州：华南理工大学出版社，2005.

[17] 谈芳，朱慧萍. 外经贸英语函电[M]. 上海：学林出版社，2005.

[18] 邹建华，江峰. 实用进出口英语函电[M]. 北京：电子工业出版社，2005.

[19] 方宁，王维平. 商务英语函电[M]. 杭州：浙江大学出版社，2004.

[20] 尹小莹. 外贸英语函电[M]. 3 版. 西安：西安交通大学出版社，2004.

[21] 齐智英. 商务英语函电[M]. 2 版. 北京：机械工业出版社，2004.

[22] 隋思忠. 外贸英语函电[M]. 大连：东北财经大学出版社，2004.

[23] 简怡. 新世纪商务英语函电[M]. 天津：天津大学出版社，2003.

[24] 凌华倍，朱佩芬. 外经贸英语函电与谈判[M]. 3 版. 北京：中国对外经济贸易出版社，2002.

[25] 王乃彦. 商务英语函电[M]. 北京：中国商务出版社，2009.

[26] 赵银德. 外贸函电[M]. 2 版. 北京：机械工业出版社，2010.

[27] 甘鸿. 外经贸英语函电[M]. 上海：上海科学技术文献出版社，1996.

[28] 陆墨珠. 国际商务函电[M]. 北京：对外经济贸易大学出版社，2005.

[29] 陈永生，赵金忠，等. 国际商务函电与合同[M]. 北京：华语教学出版社，2001.

[30] 黄水乞. 外贸英文信函范例与常用精句[M]. 广州：广东经济出版社，2011.

[31] 张爱玲，房爱群. 国际商务函电[M]. 北京：北京大学出版社，2011.

[32] 郭炳武. 外贸函电[M]. 北京：中国电力出版社，2011.

[33] 孟建国. 外贸函电（双语）[M]. 北京：中国财政经济出版社，2011.

[34] 殷秀玲. 外贸函电[M]. 上海：立信会计出版社，2011.

[35] 李卫. 外贸函电[M]. 2 版. 北京：电子工业出版社，2011.

[36] 关兵. 国际商务函电[M]. 北京：中国物资出版社，2009.

[37] 韩芹，边洁英. 国际商务英语函电[M]. 北京：北京大学出版社 2007.

[38] 李雅静，张德玉. 涉外经贸英语函电[M]. 北京：中国海洋大学出版社，2010.

[39] HELENE REY. International trade and currency exchange[J]. The review of economic studies, 2001(2): 443-464.

[40] JEAN-MARIE VIAENE, CASPER G VRIES. On the design of invoicing practices in international trade[J]. Open economies review, 1992(3): 133-142.

[41] 赵银德. 外贸函电[M]. 3 版. 北京：机械工业出版社，2016.

[42] 兰天. 外贸英语函电[M]. 8 版. 大连：东北财经大学出版社，2018.

[43] 张静，张晓云. 外贸英文函电[M]. 北京：高等教育出版社，2018.

[44] 王学惠，王可畏. 国际结算教程[M]. 北京：清华大学出版社，北京交通大学出版社，2017.

[45] 易露霞，刘洁，尤彧聪. 外贸英语函电[M]. 4 版. 北京：清华大学出版社，2020.

[46] 林涛，姜丽. 国际商务英文与函电[M]. 2 版. 北京：清华大学出版社，2018.

[47] 蔡惠伟. 外贸英语函电[M]. 北京：清华大学出版社，2019.

[48] 李蓉. 实用商务英语写作[M]. 北京：清华大学出版社，北京交通大学出版社，2017.

[49] 安锦兰，李文洁. 商务英语写作[M]. 北京：清华大学出版社，2014.

[50] 束光辉. 现代商务英语写作[M]. 北京：北京交通大学出版社，2016.

[51] 王宁. 外贸函电实务[M]. 2 版. 北京：对外经贸大学出版社，2019.

[52] 苏振东，刘莉. 外贸函电[M]. 北京：清华大学出版社，2015.

[53] 王珏. 商务写作与外贸函电[M]. 北京：中国人民大学出版社，2017.

[54] 张静，张晓云. 外贸英文函电[M]. 北京：高等教育出版社，2018.

[55] 芮燕萍. 商务英语写作[M]. 北京：高等教育出版社，2020.